eBook and Digital Learning Tools

for

Emancipation and the End of Slavery

JOEL M. SIPRESS

Carefully scratch off the silver coating with a coin to see your personal redemption code.

Scratch here to reveal your access code.
This access code may only be used by the original purchaser.

This code can be used only once and cannot be shared!

OXFORD
UNIVERSITY PRESS

D0088240

Directions
eBook and

VIA THE OUP SITE

Visit **www.oup.com/us/ debatingamericanhistory**

Select the edition you are using and the student resources for that edition.

Click the link to upgrade your access to the student resources.

Follow the on-screen instructions.

Enter your personal redemption code when prompted on the checkout screen.

VIA YOUR SCHOOL'S LEARNING MANAGEMENT SYSTEM

Log in to your instructor's course.

When you click a link to a protected resource, you will be prompted to register for access.

Follow the on-screen instructions.

Enter your personal redemption code when prompted on the checkout screen.

For assistance with code redemption or registration, please contact customer support at **arc.support@oup.com.**

PRAISE FOR *DEBATING AMERICAN HISTORY*

"*Debating American History* repositions the discipline of history as one that is rooted in discovery, investigation, and interpretation."
—Ingrid Dineen-Wimberly,
University of California, Santa Barbara

"*Debating American History* is an excellent replacement for a 'big assignment' in a course. Offering a way to add discussion to a class, it is also a perfect 'active learning' assignment, in a convenient package."
—Gene Rhea Tucker, Temple College

"The advantage that *Debating American History* has over other projects and texts currently available is that it brings a very clear and focused organization to the notion of classroom debate. The terms of each debate are clear. The books introduce students to historiography and primary sources. Most of all, the project re-envisions the way that US history should be taught. No other textbook or set of teaching materials does what these books do when taken together as the sum of their parts."
—Ian Hartman, University of Alaska

DEBATING AMERICAN HISTORY

EMANCIPATION AND THE END OF SLAVERY

DEBATING AMERICAN HISTORY

Series Editors: Joel M. Sipress, David J. Voelker

DEBATING AMERICAN HISTORY

EMANCIPATION AND THE END OF SLAVERY

Joel M. Sipress

UNIVERSITY OF WISCONSIN–SUPERIOR

NEW YORK   OXFORD

OXFORD UNIVERSITY PRESS

Oxford University Press is a department of the University of Oxford.
It furthers the University's objective of excellence in research, scholarship,
and education by publishing worldwide. Oxford is a registered trade mark of
Oxford University Press in the UK and certain other countries.

Published in the United States of America by Oxford University Press
198 Madison Avenue, New York, NY 10016, United States of America.

Library of Congress Cataloging-in-Publication Data

Names: Sipress, Joel M., author.
Title: Emancipation and the End of Slavery / Joel M. Sipress, University of
  Wisconsin-Superior.
Description: New York : Oxford University Press, 2020. | Series: Debating
  American history | Includes index.
Identifiers: LCCN 2018058940 | ISBN 9780190057077 (pbk.)
Subjects: LCSH: United States. President (1861–1865 : Lincoln). Emancipation
  Proclamation. | Slaves—Emancipation—United States—Sources. | United States—Politics
  and government—1861–1865—Sources.
Classification: LCC E453 .S57 2020 | DDC 973.7/14—dc23
LC record available at https://lccn.loc.gov/2018058940

Printing number: 9 8 7 6 5 4 3 2 1
Printed by LSC Communications, Inc., United States of America

TABLE OF CONTENTS

LIST OF MAPS AND FIGURES

Maps

Figures

ABOUT THE AUTHOR

Joel M. Sipress received his PhD in United States history from the University of North Carolina at Chapel Hill. He is a Professor of History at the University of Wisconsin–Superior, where he teaches US and Latin American History. He has published articles and book chapters on the history of the US South, with a focus on the role of race and class in late nineteenth-century southern politics. He has also written essays on teaching and learning history, including "Why Students Don't Get Evidence and What We Can Do About It," *The History Teacher* 37 (May 2004): 351–363; and "The End of the History Survey Course: The Rise and Fall of the Coverage Model," coauthored with David J. Voelker, *Journal of American History* 97 (March 2011): 1050–1066, which won the 2012 Maryellen Weimer Scholarly Work on Teaching and Learning Award. He serves as co-editor of *Debating American History* with David J. Voelker.

ACKNOWLEDGMENTS

We owe gratitude to Aeron Haynie, Regan Gurung, and Nancy Chick for introducing us and pairing us to work on the Signature Pedagogies project many years ago, as well as to the UW System's Office of Professional and Instructional Development (OPID), which supported that endeavor. Brian Wheel, formerly with Oxford University Press, helped us develop the idea for *Debating American History* and started the project rolling. We want to thank Charles Cavaliere at Oxford for taking on the project and seeing it through to publication, and Anna Russell for her excellent production work. Joel thanks the University of Wisconsin–Superior for support from a sabbatical, and David thanks the University of Wisconsin–Green Bay for support from a Research Scholar grant. David would also like to thank his colleagues in humanities, history, and First Nations Studies, who have been supportive of this project for many years, and Joel thanks his colleagues in the Department of Social Inquiry. We are also indebted to our colleagues (too numerous to mention) who have advanced the Scholarship of Teaching and Learning within the field of history. Without their efforts, this project would not have been possible. The author would also like to thank the following reviewers: Luke Harlow, University of Tennessee, Knoxville; Matthew Pinsker, Dickinson College; Tyina Steptoe, University of Arizona; Daniel Vivian, University of Louisville; Philip Levy, University of South Florida; Ingrid Dineen-Wimberly , U of Calif., Santa Barbara and U of La Verne; Kristin Hargrove, Grossmont College; Melanie Beals Goan, University of Kentucky; Paul Hart, Texas State University; Ross A. Kennedy, Illinois State University; Scott Laderman, University of Minnesota, Duluth; John Putnam, San Diego State University; Matt Tribbe, University of Houston; Linda Tomlinson, Fayetteville State University; Shauna Hann, United States Military Academy; Michael Holm, Boston University; Raymond J. Krohn, Boise State University; Joseph Locke, University of Houston-Victoria; Ted Moore, Salt Lake Community College; Andrew L. Slap, East Tennessee State University; Matthew J. Clavin, University of Houston; Amani Marshall, Georgia State University; Melanie Benson Taylor, Dartmouth College; Todd Romero, University of Houston; Robert J. Allison, Suffolk University, Boston and; Joshua Fulton, Moraine Valley Community College.

SERIES INTRODUCTION

Although history instruction has grown richer and more varied over the past few decades, many college-level history teachers remain wedded to the coverage model, whose overriding design principle is to cover huge swaths of history, largely through the use of textbooks and lectures. The implied rationale supporting the coverage model is that students must be exposed to a wide array of facts, narratives, and concepts to have the necessary background both to be effective citizens and to study history at a more advanced level—something that few students actually undertake. Although coverage-based courses often afford the opportunity for students to encounter primary sources, the imperative to cover an expansive body of material dominates these courses; and the main assessment technique, whether implemented through objective or written exams, is to require students to identify or reproduce authorized knowledge.

Unfortunately, the coverage model has been falling short of its own goals since its very inception in the late nineteenth century. Educators and policymakers have been lamenting the historical ignorance of American youth going back to at least 1917, as Stanford professor of education Sam Wineburg documented in his illuminating exposé of the history of standardized tests of historical knowledge.[1] In 2010, the *New York Times* declared that "History is American students' worst subject," basing this judgment on yet another round of abysmal standardized test scores.[2] As we have documented in our own historical research, college professors over the past century have episodically criticized the coverage model and offered alternatives. Recently, however, college-level history instructors have been forming a scholarly community to improve the teaching of the introductory course by doing research that includes rigorous analysis of student learning. A number of historians who have become involved in this discipline-based pedagogical

---

1   Sam Wineburg, "Crazy for History," *Journal of American History* 90 (March 2004): 1401–1414.
2   Sam Dillon, "U.S. Students Remain Poor at History, Tests Show," *New York Times*, June 14, 2011. Accessed online at http://www.nytimes.com/2011/06/15/education/15history.html?emc=eta1&pagewanted=print.

research, known as the Scholarship of Teaching and Learning (SoTL), have begun to mount a challenge to the coverage model.[3]

Not only has the coverage model often achieved disappointing results by its own standards, it also proves ineffective at helping students learn how to think historically, which has long been a stated goal of history education. As Lendol Calder argued in a seminal 2006 article, the coverage model works to "cover up" or "conceal" the nature of historical thinking.[4] The eloquent lecture or the unified textbook narrative reinforces the idea that historical knowledge consists of a relatively straightforward description of the past. Typical methods of covering content hide from students not only the process of historical research—the discovery and interpretation of sources—but also the ongoing and evolving discussions among historians about historical meaning. In short, the coverage model impedes historical thinking by obscuring the fact that history is a complex, interpretative, and argumentative discourse.

Informed by the scholarship of the processes of teaching and learning, contemporary reformers have taken direct aim at the assumption that factual and conceptual knowledge must precede more sophisticated forms of historical study. Instead, reformers stress that students must learn to think historically by doing—at a novice level—what expert historians do.[5]

With these ideas in mind, we thus propose an argument-based model for teaching the introductory history course. In the argument-based model, students participate in a contested, evidence-based discourse about the human past. In other words, students are asked to argue about history. And by arguing, students develop the dispositions and habits of mind that are central to the discipline of history.[6] As the former American Historical Association (AHA) president Kenneth Pomeranz noted in late 2013, historians should consider seeing general education history courses as valuable "not for the sake of 'general

---

3   See Lendol Calder, "Uncoverage: Toward a Signature Pedagogy for the History Survey," *Journal of American History* 92 (March 2006): 1358–1370; Joel M. Sipress and David J. Voelker, "The End of the History Survey Course: The Rise and Fall of the Coverage Model," *Journal of American History* 97 (March 2011): 1050–1066; and Penne Restad, "American History Learned, Argued, and Agreed Upon," in Michael Sweet and Larry K. Michaelson, eds., *Team-Based Learning in the Social Sciences and Humanities*, 159–180 (Sterling, VA: Stylus, 2012). For an overview of the Scholarship of Teaching and Learning (SoTL) in history, see Joel M. Sipress and David Voelker, "From Learning History to Doing History: Beyond the Coverage Model," in *Exploring Signature Pedagogies: Approaches to Teaching Disciplinary Habits of Mind*, pp. 19–35, edited by Regan Gurung, Nancy Chick, and Aeron Haynie (Stylus Publishing, 2008). Note also that the International Society for the Scholarship of Teaching and Learning in History was formed in 2006. See http://www.indiana.edu/~histsotl/blog/.

4   Calder, "Uncoverage," 1362–1363.

5   For influential critiques of the "facts first" assumption, see Sam Wineburg, "Crazy for History," *Journal of American History* 90 (March 2004), 1401–1414; and Calder, "Uncoverage."

6   For discussions of argument-based courses, see Barbara E. Walvoord and John R. Breihan, "Arguing and Debating: Breihan's History Course," in Barbara E. Walvoord and Lucille P. McCarthy, *Thinking and Writing in College: A Naturalistic Study of Students in Four Disciplines* (Urbana, IL: National Council of Teachers of English, 1990), 97–143; Todd Estes, "Constructing the Syllabus: Devising a Framework for Helping Students Learn to Think Like Historians," *History Teacher* 40 (February 2007), 183–201; Joel M. Sipress, "Why Students Don't Get Evidence and What We Can Do About It," *The History Teacher* 37 (May 2004), 351–363; and David J. Voelker, "Assessing Student Understanding in Introductory Courses: A Sample Strategy," *The History Teacher* 41 (August 2008): 505–518.

knowledge' but for the intellectual operations you can teach."[7] Likewise, the AHA "Tuning Project" defines the discipline in a way much more consistent with an argument-based course than with the coverage model:

> History is a set of evolving rules and tools that allows us to interpret the past with clarity, rigor, and an appreciation for interpretative debate. It requires evidence, sophisticated use of information, and a deliberative stance to explain change and continuity over time. As a profoundly public pursuit, history is essential to active and empathetic citizenship and requires effective communication to make the past accessible to multiple audiences. As a discipline, history entails a set of professional ethics and standards that demand peer review, citation, and toleration for the provisional nature of knowledge."[8]

We have designed *Debating American History* with these values in mind.

In the coverage-based model, historical knowledge is seen as an end in itself. In the argument-based model, by contrast, the historical knowledge that students must master serves as a body of evidence to be employed in argument and debate. While the ultimate goal of the coverage approach is the development of a kind of cultural literacy, the argument-based history course seeks to develop historical modes of thinking and to encourage students to incorporate these modes of thinking into their daily lives. Particularly when housed within a broader curriculum that emphasizes engaged learning, an argument-based course prepares students to ask useful questions in the face of practical problems and challenges—whether personal, professional, or civic. On encountering a historical claim, such as those that frequently arise in political discussions, they will know how to ask important questions about context, evidence, and logic. In this way, the argument-based course fulfills the discipline's longstanding commitment to the cultivation of engaged and informed citizens.[9]

While there is no single correct way to structure an argument-based course, such courses do share a number of defining characteristics that drive course design.[10] In particular, argument-based courses include these elements:

1. THEY ARE ORGANIZED AROUND SIGNIFICANT HISTORICAL QUESTIONS ABOUT WHICH HISTORIANS THEMSELVES DISAGREE.

Argument-based courses are, first and foremost, question-driven courses in which "big" historical questions (rather than simply topics or themes) provide the overall organizational structure. A "big" historical question is one about which historians themselves

---

7   Kenneth Pomeranz, "Advanced History for Beginners: Why We Should Bring What's Best about the Discipline into the Gen Ed Classroom," *Perspectives on History* (November 2013), at http://www.historians.org/publications-and-directories/perspectives-on-history/november-2013/advanced-history-for-beginners-why-we-should-bring-whats-best-about-the-discipline-into-the-gen-ed-classroom.

8   This definition reflects the state of the Tuning Project as of September 2013. For more information, see "AHA History Tuning Project: 2013 History Discipline Core," at https://www.historians.org/teaching-and-learning/tuning-the-history-discipline/2013-history-discipline-core. Accessed January 31, 2019.

9   As recently as 2006, the AHA's Teaching Division reasserted the importance of history study and scholarship in the development of globally aware citizens. Patrick Manning, "Presenting History to Policy Makers: Three Position Papers," *Perspectives: The Newsmagazine of the American Historical Association* 44 (March 2006), 22–24.

10 Our approach to course design is deeply influenced by Grant Wiggins and Jay McTighe, *Understanding by Design*, 2nd ed. (Upper Saddle River, NJ: Pearson Education, 2006).

disagree and that has broad academic, intellectual, or cultural implications. Within these very broad parameters, the types of questions around which a course may be organized can vary greatly. The number of "big" questions addressed, however, must be relatively limited in number (perhaps three to five over the course of a typical fifteen-week semester), so that students can pursue the questions in depth.

2. THEY SYSTEMATICALLY EXPOSE STUDENTS TO RIVAL POSITIONS ABOUT WHICH THEY MUST MAKE INFORMED JUDGMENTS.

Argument-based courses systematically expose students to rival positions about which they must form judgments. Through repeated exploration of rival positions on a series of big questions, students see historical debate modeled in way that shatters any expectation that historical knowledge is clear-cut and revealed by authority. Students are thus confronted with the inescapable necessity to engage, consider, and ultimately evaluate the merits of a variety of perspectives.

3. THEY ASK STUDENTS TO JUDGE THE RELATIVE MERITS OF RIVAL POSITIONS ON BASIS OF HISTORICAL EVIDENCE.

To participate in historical argument, students must understand historical argument as more than a matter of mere opinion. For this to happen, students must learn to employ evidence as the basis for evaluating historical claims. Through being repeatedly asked to judge the relative merits of rival positions on the basis of evidence, students learn to see the relationship between historical evidence and historical assertions.

4. THEY REQUIRE STUDENTS TO DEVELOP THEIR OWN POSITIONS FOR WHICH THEY MUST ARGUE ON THE BASIS OF HISTORICAL EVIDENCE.

In an argument-based course, the ultimate aspiration should be for students to bring their own voices to bear on historical discourse in a way that is thoroughly grounded in evidence. Students must therefore have the opportunity to argue for their own positions. Such positions may parallel or synthesize those of the scholars with which they have engaged in the course or they may be original. In either case, though, students must practice applying disciplinary standards of evidence.

Learning to argue about history is, above all, a process that requires students to develop new skills, dispositions, and habits of mind. Students develop these attributes through the act of arguing in a supportive environment where the instructor provides guidance and feedback. The instructor is also responsible for providing students with the background, context, and in-depth materials necessary both to fully understand and appreciate each big question and to serve as the body of evidence that forms the basis for judgments and arguments. While argument-based courses eschew any attempt to provide comprehensive coverage, they ask students to think deeply about a smaller number of historical questions—and in the process of arguing about the selected questions, students will develop significant content knowledge in the areas emphasized.

While a number of textbooks and readers in American history incorporate elements of historical argumentation, there are no published materials available that are specifically designed to support an argument-based course. *Debating American History* consists of a series of modular units, each focused on a specific topic and question in American history that will support all four characteristics of an argument-based course noted previously. Instructors will select units that support their overall course design, perhaps incorporating one or two modules into an existing course or structuring an entire course around three to five such units. (Instructors, of course, are free to supplement the modular units with other materials of their choosing, such as additional primary documents, secondary articles, multimedia materials, and book chapters.) By focusing on a limited number of topics, students will be able to engage in in-depth historical argumentation, including consideration of multiple positions and substantial bodies of evidence.

Each unit has the following elements:

1. THE BIG QUESTION

A brief narrative introduction that poses the central question of the unit and provides general background.

2. HISTORIANS' CONVERSATIONS

This section establishes the debate by providing two or three original essays that present distinct and competing scholarly positions on the Big Question. While these essays make occasional reference to major scholars in the field, they are not intended to provide historiographical overviews but rather to provide models of historical argumentation through the presentation and analysis of evidence.

3. DEBATING THE QUESTION

Each module includes a variety of materials containing evidence for students to use to evaluate the various positions and develop a position of their own. Materials may include primary source documents, images, a timeline, maps, or brief secondary sources. The specific materials vary depending on the nature of the question. Some modules include detailed case studies that focus on a particular facet of the Big Question.

For example, one module that we have developed for an early American history course focuses on the following Big Question: "How were the English able to displace the thriving Powhatan people from their Chesapeake homelands in the seventeenth century?" The Historians' Conversations section includes two essays: "Position #1: The Overwhelming Advantages of the English"; and "Position #2: Strategic Mistakes of the Powhatans." The unit materials allow students to undertake a guided exploration of both Powhatan and English motivations and strategies. The materials include two case studies that serve specific pedagogical purposes. The first case study asks the question, "Did Pocahontas Rescue John Smith from Execution?" Answering this question requires grappling with the nature of primary sources and weighing additional evidence from secondary sources; given historians' confidence that Powhatan did adopt Smith during his captivity, the case study also raises important questions about Powhatan strategy. The second case study focuses on the 1622 surprise attack that the Powhatans (led by Opechancanough) launched against the English, posing the question, "What Was the Strategy behind the 1622 Powhatan Surprise Attack?" Students wrestle with a number of scholarly perspectives regarding Opechancanough's purpose and the effectiveness of his strategy. Overall, this unit introduces students to the use of primary sources and the process of weighing different historical interpretations. Because of Disney's 1995 film *Pocahontas*, many students begin the unit thinking that they already know about the contact between the Powhatans and the English; many of them also savor the chance to bring critical, historical thinking to bear on this subject, and doing so deepens their understanding of how American Indians responded to European colonization.

Along similar lines, the Big Question for a module on the Gilded Age asks, "Why Was Industrialization in the Late Nineteenth Century Accompanied by Such Great Social and Political Turmoil?" The materials provided allow students to explore the labor conflicts of the period as well as the Populist revolt and to draw conclusions regarding the underlying causes of the social and political upheavals. Primary sources allow students to delve into labor conflicts from the perspectives of both workers and management and to explore both Populist and anti-Populist perspectives. Three short case studies allow students to examine specific instances of social conflict in depth. A body of economic data from the late nineteenth century is also included.

Many history instructors, when presented with the argument-based model, find its goals to be compelling, but they fear that it is overly ambitious—that introductory-level students will be incapable of engaging in historical thinking at an acceptable level. But, we must ask, how well do students learn under the coverage model? Student performance varies in an argument-based course, but it varies widely in a coverage-based course as well. In our experience, most undergraduate students are capable of achieving a basic-level competence at identifying and evaluating historical interpretations and using primary and secondary sources as evidence to make basic historical arguments. We not only have evidence of this success in the form of our own grade books, but we have studied our students' learning to document the success of our approach.[11] Students can indeed learn how to think like historians at a novice level, and in doing so they will gain both an appreciation for the discipline and develop a set of critical skills and dispositions that will contribute to their overall higher education. For this to happen, however, a course must be "backward designed" to promote and develop historical thinking. As historian Lawrence Gipson (Wabash College) asked in a 1916 AHA discussion, "Will the student catch 'historical-mindedness' from his instructor like the mumps?"[12] The answer, clearly, is "no."

In addition to the modular units focused on big questions, instructors will also be provided with a brief instructors' manual, entitled "Developing an Argument-Based Course." This volume will provide instructors with guidance and advice on course development, as

---

11   See Sipress, "Why Students Don't Get Evidence," and Voelker, "Assessing Student Understanding."
12   Lawrence H. Gipson, "Method of the Elementary Course in the Small College," *The History Teacher's Magazine* 8 (April 1917), 128. (The conference discussion took place in 1916.)

well as with sample in-class exercises and assessments. Additionally, each module includes an Instructor's Manual. Together, these resources will assist instructors with the process of creating an argument-based course, whether for a relatively small class at a liberal arts college or for a large class of students at a university. These resources can be used in both face-to-face and online courses.

The purpose of *Debating American History* is to provide instructors with both the resources and strategies that they will need to design such a course. This textbook alternative leaves plenty of room for instructor flexibility; and it requires instructors to carefully choose, organize, and introduce the readings to students, as well as to coach students through the process of thinking historically, even as they deepen their knowledge and understanding of particular eras and topics.

Joel M. Sipress
Professor of History,
University of Wisconsin-Superior

David J. Voelker
Associate Professor of Humanities and History,
University of Wisconsin-Green Bay

DEBATING AMERICAN HISTORY

EMANCIPATION AND THE END OF SLAVERY

THE BIG QUESTION

HOW AND WHY DID EMANCIPATION BECOME A GOAL OF THE UNION WAR EFFORT?

On the morning of Monday, the 21st of July, 1862, Abraham Lincoln's cabinet secretaries gathered for a special meeting called by the President to consider a series of new policies for suppressing the Confederate rebellion. The meeting came at a difficult time for the Lincoln administration and for the Union war effort. Fighting had been raging for over a year, casualties were mounting, and victory was nowhere in sight. The previous spring, when Lincoln first called for volunteers to crush the rebellion, most in the North expected a quick and easy victory; but the disastrous Union defeat at the battle of Bull Run in July 1861 shattered those illusions. In the spring of 1862, federal military forces under the command of General George B. McClellan came within just a few miles of the Confederate capital of Richmond, Virginia, again raising hopes that victory was at hand. In late June, though, Confederate forces led by General Robert E. Lee launched a counterattack that drove the Union army back from Richmond; and by early July, it was clear that McClellan's campaign had ended in failure. This defeat brought despair to many in the North, as did the staggering casualty rates of the battles outside Richmond—over 30,000 Union and Confederate soldiers had been left dead or wounded.

In the wake of McClellan's defeat, Lincoln gathered his cabinet to present a set of new military measures that reflected a shift toward a "hard" war. Some of these new policies were relatively straightforward. Henceforth, for instance, Union field commanders would be authorized to seize property from Confederate sympathizers to supply federal troops as they pushed south. When the cabinet reconvened the next morning, however, Lincoln dropped a bombshell by informing the group that he planned to issue a military order declaring all persons held as slaves in Confederate territory to be forever free. This dramatic step was a sharp break with Lincoln's long-held position on the issue of slavery. Despite his moral opposition to the South's "peculiar institution," Lincoln had consistently maintained that he had neither the desire nor the authority as president to interfere with slavery in those states where it already existed. For the first year of the war, Lincoln had resisted pressure from abolitionists to use his military authority to strike a blow against slavery.

Lincoln informed his cabinet secretaries that his decision regarding emancipation was firm and not subject to debate. Secretary of State William Seward warned that the grim military situation might make the immediate issuance of an emancipation proclamation seem an act of desperation and suggested that Lincoln wait for a military success before taking action. The President accepted Seward's advice. Lincoln's opportunity arrived in September of 1862 when McClellan turned back Lee's invasion of the state of Maryland at the Battle of Antietam. On September 22 (five days after the battle), Lincoln issued a military proclamation declaring that, as of January 1, 1863, all those held as slaves in areas still in rebellion against the United States government would be "then, thenceforward, and forever free." On New Year's Day of 1863, shortly after noon, President Lincoln signed the final Emancipation Proclamation. By a stroke of a pen, nearly four million men, women, and children were declared free.

The significance of the Emancipation Proclamation lay less in its immediate impact than in the way it transformed the Civil War into a war against slavery. The Proclamation did not bring the institution of slavery to an immediate end in the United States. The so-called border states of Delaware, Maryland, Kentucky, and Missouri (slave states that had not joined the rebellion) were not covered by its provisions. (See map of the Union and Confederate States) The Confederate state of Tennessee, which by 1863 was under Union military occupation, was also exempted, as were sections of northern Virginia and South-ern Louisiana that were under federal control. In fact, outside of a few small pockets, the territories covered by the Emancipation Proclamation were beyond Lincoln's direct reach, as they lay behind Confederate lines. The Emancipation Proclamation, however, made the abolition of slavery a *goal* of the Union war effort. The Proclamation declared those held as slaves in Confederate territory to be *forever* free; and as federal armies pushed south, they thus became armies of liberation. When William Tecumseh Sherman's soldiers marched through central Georgia in 1864's famed March to the Sea, for instance, thousands of slaves

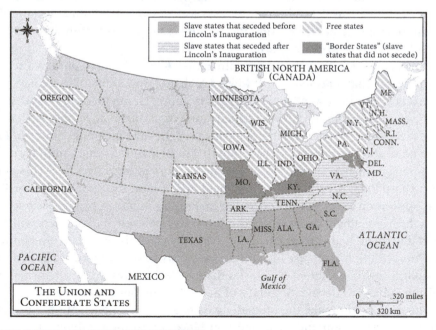

MAP 1. THE UNION AND CONFEDERATE STATES

deserted the farms and plantations in which they had been held in bondage to join the Union columns. Union forces also actively recruited liberated slaves to join the United States Army, with 179,000 black men (mostly former slaves) ultimately enlisting. By the time of the Confederate surrender in the spring of 1865, slavery was all but dead in the United States, a result confirmed by the 13th Amendment to the Constitution, which formally abolished the institution throughout the nation when it was ratified on December 6, 1865.

The emancipation of millions of African American slaves during the American Civil War was a fundamental turning point in the history of the United States. In retrospect, abolition may have seemed inevitable; but for most who lived through it, it was anything but. Although the issue of slavery, particularly its expansion into the new territories of the West, had divided the country along sectional lines, before the war, those who favored its immediate abolition had remained a minority, even in the free states of the North. Only a handful of prophetic figures, such as the great abolitionist leader Frederick Douglass, had predicted that the war might bring an end to slavery. How and why was it that emancipation so unexpectedly became a goal of the Union war effort?

In many ways, Lincoln was a surprising liberator, as emancipation contradicted the public stance he had taken on slavery throughout his career in politics. Believing that the federal government lacked the legal authority to abolish slavery in those states where it already existed, Lincoln had long advocated gradual emancipation through the voluntary action of those in the slave states, a position that put him at odds with abolitionists who advocated direct and immediate action against slavery. Skeptical about the prospects for racial equality on American soil, Lincoln supported the voluntary emigration (or "colonization") of African American people out of the United States and opposed granting black residents of his home state of Illinois such basic civil rights as the right to vote or to serve on juries. Lincoln was a vehement opponent of slavery's expansion into new territories and hoped that the restriction of the institution to the states where it already existed would place it on a path toward what he termed its "ultimate extinction." Exactly how and when this result would be achieved remained unclear, even in his own mind.

Lincoln ran for president in 1860 on a platform of restricting slavery's expansion but took great pains to assure southern slave owners that, if elected, he would take no direct action against the institution where it existed. His political opponents nevertheless portrayed Lincoln's candidacy as a grave threat to the institution of slavery. One Virginia newspaper, for instance, spoke of his "inveterate hatred of slavery and his openly avowed predilections of negro equality."[1] Following Lincoln's November 1860 election victory, political leaders in southern states began to agitate for independence (or "secession," as it was called). By the time of Lincoln's presidential inauguration the following March, a total of seven states had seceded and organized themselves into an independent southern republic deemed the Confederate States of America. In April 1861, Confederate forces in Charleston, South Carolina, opened fire on a US military outpost at Fort Sumter, prompting Lincoln to call on the remaining states to provide troops to suppress the rebellion. Four additional southern slave states refused to provide soldiers and instead passed ordinances

---

1   Quoted in Avery O. Craven, *The Growth of Southern Nationalism, 1848–1861* (Baton Rouge, LA: Louisiana State University Press, 1953), 346.

of secession and joined the Confederacy. For months afterward, it appeared that at least some of the border slave states (Missouri and Kentucky especially) might secede, as well.

Throughout the secession crisis, Lincoln took a hard line against those seeking independence from the United States. The new president insisted that secession was illegal and would not be tolerated. On the issue of slavery, however, Lincoln maintained his traditional stance. Though he refused to compromise on the question of slavery's expansion, he repeated his pledge to respect the institution where it currently existed. In his inaugural address, Lincoln declared, "I have no purpose, directly or indirectly, to interfere with the institution of slavery in the States where it exists. I believe I have no lawful right to do so, and I have no inclination to do so." For the first year of the war, Lincoln stuck to this position, despite the spread of emancipationist sentiment in the North, even among many who had previously rejected abolitionism. Lincoln was anxious to prevent the Civil War from degenerating into what he termed "a violent and remorseless revolutionary struggle."[2] The war was one to preserve the Union and nothing else, he maintained. If southern rebels set down their arms and renounced secession, the nation would be restored as it was.

Lincoln's July 1862 decision to declare those held as slaves within rebel territory to be forever free was a radical departure from his previous position on slavery—a position he had maintained consistently throughout a career in public life. Why, then, did he do it? Why, after repeatedly declaring that the sole goal of the war was to preserve the Union, did Lincoln transform the Civil War into a struggle to both preserve the Union *and* to abolish slavery? The failure to quickly and decisively suppress the rebellion provided the context for this momentous decision, but that alone does not explain *why* he did it. To what extent did his personal anti-slavery convictions play a role? What was the impact of growing abolitionist sentiment in the North? When asked later, the President explained that he acted out of military necessity. What was that necessity, and was that truly the motivating factor?

Some have suggested that Lincoln was pushed to his decision by forces beyond his control. A month into the Civil War, former slave and abolitionist Frederick Douglass predicted that the war for the Union would inevitably become a war against slavery:

> *The American people and the Government at Washington may refuse to recognize it for a time; but the "inexorable logic of events" will force it upon them in the end; that the war now being waged in this land is a war for and against slavery; and that it can never be effectually put down till one or the other of these vital forces is completely destroyed.*[3]

And, indeed, as Douglass predicted, the outbreak of hostilities between Union and Confederate forces began immediately to weaken the bonds that kept millions of black southerners enslaved. Just weeks after the bombardment of Fort Sumter (the first battle of the war), three slaves who were employed building Confederate fortifications in coastal Virginia escaped to Union lines. Over the next year, thousands of others followed in their

---

2   Abraham Lincoln, "Annual Message to Congress," December 3, 1861, in *Collected Works of Abraham Lincoln,* vol. 5, ed. Roy P. Basler (New Brunswick, NJ: Rutgers University Press, 1953), 49.

3   "Nemesis," *Douglass' Monthly* (Rochester, New York), May 1861.

footsteps, as Union encampments became magnets for enslaved African Americans seeking to escape from bondage.

The Lincoln Administration had little choice but to confront the issue of slavery, if for no other reason than to clarify the status of escaped slaves. In normal times, the army would have been legally obliged to return runaways to their owners. Military officers, however, were reluctant to do so, whether out of moral qualms or their knowledge that slave labor was central to the Confederate war effort. For months, the President and the Congress struggled to determine federal policy toward runaway slaves. At first, the question was simply whether those who had escaped to Union lines should be declared to be free. As the numbers of runaways swelled, though, calls for a general proclamation of emancipation that would apply to all slaves within the Confederacy grew, as did demands that freed slaves be allowed to enlist in the Union army. Meanwhile, pro-slavery Unionists warned that a general declaration of emancipation would alienate Union supporters in the border states (slave states like Kentucky and Missouri that had refused to secede). This too, was part of the context for Lincoln's decision to issue the Emancipation Proclamation.

When President Lincoln decided in favor of emancipation, to what extent was he acting on his own personal values and beliefs to make history? To what extent was he simply reacting to forces that were beyond his control, including the force of thousands of enslaved African Americans who sought freedom behind Union lines? The debate among historians regarding emancipation raises profound questions about how historical changes, such as the abolition of slavery, come to pass. Do so-called great men like Abraham Lincoln who make history? Or is history made through the countless everyday decisions of so-called ordinary people—ordinary people like those held in bondage who took the opportunities provided by the war to pursue their own freedom?

TIMELINE

1860 (November)
Abraham Lincoln elected President on a promise to halt the expansion of slavery into new territories. Reassures southern slave owners that he will not interfere with the institution in states where it currently existed.

1861 (March 4)
Lincoln inaugurated President. Reaffirms that he will not interfere with the institution of slavery where it already existed but declares the Union to be indivisible.

1861 (May 23)
Three slaves employed building Confederate fortifications in coastal Virginia escape to Union lines at Fortress Monroe. Federal commander Benjamin Butler declares the men to be "contraband of war" and refuses to return them to their owner. In the months that follow, thousands of slaves flee to federal lines at Fortress Monroe and elsewhere.

1860 (December 20)
South Carolina secedes from the United States.

1861 (April 12)
Confederate forces in Charleston, South Carolina, launch attack on the federal military installation at Fort Sumter. Lincoln issues call for troops to suppress the rebellion.

1861 (August 6)
The First Confiscation Act, which voided slave masters ownership rights over slaves employed in support of the rebellion, becomes law.

1861 (January–February)
Six additional lower south states secede.

1861 (April–June)
Four additional Upper South states secede and join the Confederacy.

1861 (August 30)
General John C. Frémont declares the slaves of all rebel slave owners in the state of Missouri to be free. Lincoln overrules Fremont.

1861 (December 3)
Lincoln asks Congress to provide funds to encourage the voluntary emigration of freed slaves from the United States.

1862 (March 6)
Lincoln asks Congress to provide compensation to slave owners in states that agree to gradually abolish slavery.

1862 (March 10)
Lincoln meets with representatives of border states (slave states that had not seceded) and urges them to pursue gradual compensated emancipation within their states.

1862 (May 9)
General David Hunter declares all slaves in the Confederate states of Georgia, Florida, and South Carolina to be forever free. Lincoln overrules Hunter.

1862 (June 25–July 1)
General George B. McClellan's campaign to capture the Confederate capital of Richmond, Virginia, is defeated at the Seven Days battles. A wave of pessimism sweeps the North.

1862 (July 17)
The Second Confiscation Act, which declared free all slaves who came within Union lines whose owners were engaged in rebellion, becomes law.

1862 (July 22)
Lincoln informs his cabinet of his intent to issue a military order declaring all those held in slavery in rebel areas to be forever free. Secretary of State William H. Seward advises Lincoln to wait for a military victory to issue the order.

1862 (September 17)
Confederate invasion of Maryland halted at Battle of Antietam.

1862 (September 22)
Lincoln issues the Preliminary Emancipation Proclamation.

1863 (January 1)
Lincoln issues the final Emancipation Proclamation.

1865
The 13th Amendment to the United States Constitution, which abolished slavery throughout the nation, is ratified.

HISTORIANS' CONVERSATIONS

POSITION #1—A GROWING TIDE OF FREEDOM

The African American Role in Emancipation

On May 23, 1861, six weeks after the Confederate assault on Fort Sumter in Charleston Harbor, three slaves in coastal Virginia escaped to federal lines at Fortress Monroe. (Map 1, "The Union and Confederate States.") At the time, President Lincoln was desperate to persuade southern slave owners that his administration posed no threat to the region's "peculiar institution." His sole goal, Lincoln insisted, was to suppress the rebellion and preserve the Union. If Confederates would simply lay down their arms and drop their bid for independence, the President promised, the Union as it had been could be restored with slavery intact where it already existed. The three men who escaped to Fortress Monroe, however, understood what Lincoln did not—that the outbreak of hostilities between Union and Confederate forces would inevitably undermine the system of slavery and the authority of slave owners. Those in bondage did not wait for an invitation to pursue their freedom. Rather, countless thousands followed in the footsteps of those initial three and seized the opportunity for liberation provided by the war. By doing so, they forced the issue of emancipation on the Lincoln administration's agenda. As historian Barbara Fields writes, "It was they who taught the nation that it must place the abolition of slavery at the head of its agenda."[1]

Lincoln, by contrast, resisted the growing tide of freedom. Despite his moral opposition to slavery, the President's highest priority in the early stages of the war was to counter the secessionist wave engulfing the South and to unify northerners behind the war effort. Lincoln was particularly concerned to maintain the loyalty of the border slave states of Delaware, Maryland, Kentucky, and Missouri, without which it would be difficult or impossible to suppress the rebellion. To mobilize white support for a war to preserve the Union, particularly in the border states, Lincoln had to demonstrate his commitment to maintaining the institution of slavery where it already existed. This he did, for instance, by overturning General John C. Frémont's August 1861 proclamation declaring all slaves of rebel owners in the state of Missouri to be forever free. Lincoln, however, could not prevent the enslaved (both in the border and Confederate states) from seeking freedom at Union encampments.

---

1 Barbara J. Fields, "Who Freed the Slaves?" in *The Civil War: An Illustrated History*, Geoffrey C. Ward with Ric Burns and Ken Burns (New York: Alfred A. Knopf, 1990), 179.

As their numbers grew, northerners increasingly came to understand that a war for the Union must inevitably become a war against slavery; and that by embracing the cause of emancipation, those seeking freedom could be made a powerful force for the Union. Ultimately, Lincoln did come to accept what the slaves by their own actions had already demonstrated—that a war for the Union must by necessity become a war for human freedom.

The arrival of those first three men at Fortress Monroe in May of 1861 illustrates the overall dynamics of emancipation. The federal commander at Fort Monroe, General Benjamin F. Butler, was a prominent Democratic politician from Massachusetts who had not previously displayed particular sympathy for the plight of the enslaved—and had, in fact, been a vocal critic of abolitionism. Butler, though, was now confronted not by the abstract issue of slavery but by three flesh and blood human beings. Butler faced a difficult dilemma. Under federal law, he was obliged to return fugitive slaves to their masters; yet doing so would aid the enemy war effort, as they had informed him that they were about to be taken to "Carolina" to provide labor to the Confederate military. Furthermore, Butler was aware that Confederate forces in the vicinity of Fort Monroe were making extensive use of slave labor to construct fortifications. Having no authority to free the men, Butler instead declared them to be "contraband of war," and he refused to honor demands from their master that they be returned. As news spread of Butler's decision, more fugitive slaves arrived at Fortress Monroe, including men, women, and children. With the approval of his superiors, Butler employed the men as paid military laborers. As a humanitarian gesture, the former opponent of abolitionism allowed the women and children to remain as refugees. By the end of July, over 850 escaped slaves had taken refuge at Fort Monroe. Over the course of the war, Butler switched his political allegiances to the Republican Party (the party of Lincoln) and became a fierce advocate of emancipation and black civil rights.

Similar scenes were played out wherever federal forces were to be found in the first year of the war, as thousands of enslaved African Americans escaped to Union lines. Their growing numbers finally forced the Congress to act. In August of 1861, the Congress gave legislative sanction to Butler's "contraband" policy in the First Confiscation Act, which forfeited the property rights of masters whose slaves had been employed in support of the rebellion. On the ground, however, emancipation had already proceeded far beyond the provisions of the Confiscation Act. Federal officers were often unable to determine who among the growing number fugitives had been employed by the Confederate military. In many cases, commanders simply allowed all who arrived at their encampments to remain while employing as many possible in roles ranging from cooks, to orderlies, to military laborers.

As Union soldiers encountered the growing numbers of fugitives in their midst, attitudes toward slavery began to change. "By abandoning their owners, coming uninvited into Union lines, and offering their lives and labor in the Federal cause," writes historian Ira Berlin, "slaves forced Federal soldiers at the lowest level to recognize their importance to the Union's success." As the Union army pushed into the South, emancipationist sentiments became more pronounced. It was one thing to consider the moral dilemma of slavery from the security of a farmstead in Illinois or Vermont. It was quite another to witness the conditions of slavery firsthand, to see the extraordinary lengths to which fugitive slaves went to gain their freedom, to interact with them on a daily basis in camp, and to see some forcibly returned to the scenes of their bondage. As historian Chandra Manning points out, it was soldiers who "forged the crucial link" between slaves, who forced emancipation onto the Union agenda, and the decision makers who would ultimately declare emancipation to be federal policy. "Slaves convinced enlisted soldiers, who modified their beliefs and their behavior," she writes. "In turn," Manning explains, "the men of the rank and file used letters, camp newspapers, and their own actions to influence the opinions of civilians and leaders."[2]

As abolitionist sentiment spread through the army, the military leadership began to push for bolder policies regarding slavery. In November 1861, Secretary of War Simon Cameron included a proposal in his annual report that enslaved men capable of military service who came within Union lines should be enlisted in the army. At the insistence of the President, the recommendation was removed from the document's final version—though, much to Lincoln's annoyance, the original language did become public. At about the same time, the navy began to quietly enroll African American recruits, and the army began to employ escaped slaves in quasi-military roles along the South Carolina coast. In March 1862, Congress barred the military from returning any runaway to bondage (whether in the Confederate states or border slave states), thus resolving the lingering ambiguity regarding the obligations of officers to enforce the federal fugitive slave law. In the same month, an abolitionist general named David Hunter took command of Union operations along the South Carolina coast. Hunter began to quietly organize the area's significant slave population into military units. When Hunter took the further step of declaring slavery abolished in South Carolina, Georgia, and Florida, his pronouncement was immediately overturned by President Lincoln.

Gradually, the President came to recognize that despite his own intentions, the war itself had undermined the authority of slave owners and had emboldened slaves to seek their freedom; and that by doing so, the conflict had begun to call slavery's future into question. In his March 1862 message to Congress advocating gradual emancipation, he warned that if the rebellion continued, more sweeping measures than those he had sought to avoid might become unavoidable. Two months later, in rescinding Hunter's emancipation order, he again urged acceptance of his gradual emancipation plan and implied that a broader order of military emancipation might become necessary. On July 12, in his final appeal to border state representatives to accept his gradual emancipation proposal, Lincoln warned that if the war were to long continue, slavery in those states would be extinguished by "mere friction and abrasion—by the mere incidents of the war." Lincoln urged them to accept gradual emancipation as an alternative to the more catastrophic alternative that was sure to follow were the war to continue.[3]

In many places, the institution of slavery had been brought to the brink of collapse by July 1862 through the actions of thousands of individual men and women who risked

2   Ira Belin, "Who Freed the Slaves? Emancipation and Its Meaning," in *Union & Emancipation: Essays on Politics and Race in the Civil War Era*, eds. David W. Blight and Brooks D. Simpson (Kent, OH: Kent State University Press, 1997), 110; Chandra Manning, *What This Cruel War Was Over: Soldiers, Slavery, and the Civil War* (New York: Alfred A. Knopf, 2007), 13.

3   Lincoln, Appeal to Border State Representatives to Favor Compensated Emancipation, in *The Collected Works of Abraham Lincoln*, ed. Roy P. Basler, vol. 5 (New Brunswick, NJ: Rutgers University Press, 1953), 317–319.

all to seek freedom behind Union lines. And, by that time, the heroism of these men and women had persuaded much of the military, including many in positions of high leadership, that a war for the Union had to become a war for human freedom, and that the slaves themselves must be enlisted in that cause not just as laborers and sympathizers but as active combatants. As Barbara Fields writes, "By the time Lincoln had issued his Emancipation Proclamation, no human being alive could have held back the tide that swept toward freedom."[4] Slaves were not, of course, solely responsible for their own liberation. Northern abolitionists and anti-slavery congressional leaders certainly pushed Lincoln to recognize the inevitability of emancipation. Key military leaders like Benjamin Butler and David Hunter, by recognizing the humanity of enslaved African Americans and seeing how they might contribute to the war effort, created more favorable circumstances for individuals to escape to freedom. As Ira Berlin points out, though, it was the enslaved people themselves who were the "prime movers" in the emancipation drama: "Slaves set others in motion, including many who would never have moved if left to their own devices."[5] It was slaves who acted first to force attention to the issue of freedom in ways that could not be ignored. It was slaves who demonstrated the fragility of the South's "peculiar institution" and the potential value of black labor, both in combat and otherwise, to the cause of the Union. It was slaves who proved their full humanity to Union soldiers and won new converts to the abolitionist cause. In doing all these things, the enslaved demonstrated the power of ordinary people, even those forced to live under the most extreme and dehumanizing forms of oppression, to make history.

---

4   Fields, "Who Freed the Slaves?," 181.
5   Berlin, "Who Freed the Slaves?," 112.

POSITION #2—THE CAUTIOUS ABOLITIONIST

Abraham Lincoln and the End of Slavery

Beginning in the 1960s and 1970s, a new generation of historians came of age who emphasized the role of ordinary people in the making of history. Previous historians, they argued, had overstated the historical role of "great men" to the exclusion of ordinary men and women. This new perspective among historians brought needed attention to the experiences and the contributions of previously neglected groups—such as women, immigrants, and slaves—as well as to those of everyday working people of all races and ethnicities. At times, though, the new focus on "history from the bottom up" simply took the old top-down approach and flipped it on its head, producing new scholarship that was as one-dimensional as the old scholarship that it replaced. Take, for instance, the question of Abraham Lincoln and emancipation. Historians have long known that the popular image of Lincoln as the "great emancipator" was overly simplistic. Many factors (and many actors) contributed to the demise of slavery in the United States. Among the new historians, however, Lincoln risks being pushed to the edge of the emancipation story entirely by an overemphasis on the role of slaves themselves in securing their own freedom. Vincent Harding, for instance, discounts Lincoln's role in the destruction of slavery as largely mythical. "While the concrete historical realities of the time testified to the costly, daring, and courageous activities of hundreds of thousands of black people breaking loose from slavery and setting themselves free," writes Harding, "the myth gave the credit for this freedom to a white Republican president."[1]

The new historians are to be thanked for shining a light on the role that slaves played in their own liberation. Nonetheless, the new history goes too far in its attempt to strip from Lincoln the title of emancipator. Although Abraham Lincoln had a deeply held moral opposition to the institution of slavery, he was also a realist who recognized that a direct assault on slavery would achieve little except backlash and strife. Lincoln was, in the words of Richard Striner, "a fervent idealist endowed with a remarkable gift for strategy." Prior

---

1   Quoted in James M. McPherson, *Drawn with the Sword: Reflections on the American Civil War* (New York: Oxford University Press, 1996), 195. See also Lerone Bennett Jr., *Forced into Glory: Abraham Lincoln's White Dream* (Chicago: Johnson Publishing Company, 2000). For a more nuanced version of the "self-emancipation" argument, see Ira Belin, "Who Freed the Slaves? Emancipation and Its Meaning," in *Union & Emancipation: Essays on Politics and Race in the Civil War Era*, eds. David W. Blight and Brooks D. Simpson (Kent, OH: Kent State University Press, 1997), 105–121.

to the Civil War, Lincoln believed that arresting the expansion of slavery and promoting its gradual and voluntary abolition within the individual states was the best long-term strategy for bringing an end to the institution. With the outbreak of hostilities, he began to conceive of bolder action. "His goals kept expanding as he tested how far he might go in his attempt to change history," writes Striner.[2] Finally, in the fall of 1862, when he saw the opportunity to move toward the rapid destruction of slavery, Lincoln issued a general proclamation of emancipation and made abolition a goal of the Union war effort.

"If slavery is not wrong, nothing is wrong," wrote Lincoln in 1864. "I can not remember when I did not so think, and feel."[3] The historical record confirms Lincoln's recollection. What little documentation we have of Lincoln's early views on slavery demonstrates his moral opposition to the institution. Until the passage of the Kansas-Nebraska Act in 1854, though, Lincoln did not make the issue of slavery a priority in his public life. Rather, like many northerners, he tolerated slavery's existence in the southern states in the belief that the nation was on a path toward its gradual abolition. The Kansas-Nebraska Act, which overturned the 1820 Missouri Compromise and its prohibition against slavery in the territories of the northern Great Plains, changed all that. Faced with the expansion of slavery into territories from which it had been previously been banned, Lincoln made the containment and eventual elimination of the institution the centerpiece of his political activities. Lincoln's views were best summed up in his famous "House Divided" speech of 1858. The nation, he explained, could not permanently endure half slave and half free. Either the expansion of slavery would be arrested and the public mind satisfied that it was on the course of what Lincoln termed its "ultimate extinction," or the advocates of slavery would push it forward until it became legal throughout the United States.[4] Yet, even as Lincoln envisioned the ultimate extinction of slavery, he was careful to assure southern slave owners that he had no desire, nor did he believe the federal government had the power, to directly interfere with the institution of slavery where it already existed. The surest and safest path to the abolition of slavery, in Lincoln's view, was gradual and with the acquiescence of southern slave owners. Too hasty and forceful a push for abolition would result in nothing but chaos, turmoil, and defiant resistance. Lincoln's gradualism rested on a firm belief that history was on his side, with slavery in retreat across the western hemisphere, a trend exemplified by the institution's abolition in the British colonies in the Caribbean in the early 1830s.

The position on slavery that Lincoln articulated in the 1850s remained consistent through the 1860 presidential campaign and the secession crisis. In the wake of Lincoln's election, as several lower South states moved toward secession, members of Congress worked frantically to find a compromise that might resolve the crisis. While Lincoln expressed openness to a variety of compromise measures (including stringent enforcement of the requirement that fugitive slaves be returned into bondage), on the issue of slavery's

---

2   Richard Striner, *Father Abraham: Lincoln's Relentless Struggle to End Slavery* (New York: Oxford University Press, 2006), 2–3.

3   Lincoln to Albert G. Hodges, April 4, 1864, in *The Collected Works of Abraham Lincoln*, ed. Roy P. Basler, vol. 7 (New Brunswick, NJ: Rutgers University Press, 1953), 281.

4   Lincoln, "A House Divided": Speech at Springfield, Illinois, in *The Collected Works of Abraham Lincoln*, ed. Roy P. Basler, vol. 2 (New Brunswick: Rutgers University Press, 1953), 461–462.

expansion he was, in his own words, "inflexible."[5] In the period between his election and his inauguration, Lincoln worked tirelessly to prevent Republican congressional leaders from embracing any compromise that would allow for the expansion of slavery beyond the states where it was already legal. At the same time, he continued to assure southern slave owners that he had neither the intention nor the authority to interfere with slavery where it already existed. In the absence of a compromise on the territorial issue, Lincoln's assurances proved insufficient to placate southern secessionists. The result was war.

While Lincoln maintained his same basic stance on slavery into the first year of the war, within the framework of gradual and voluntary abolition, he pursued unprecedented steps in support of freedom. In August 1861, Lincoln signed into law the First Confiscation Act, which allowed for the confiscation of slaves who were employed in the service of the rebellion. Though the law did not explicitly emancipate any slave, it did establish the principle that in the context of the rebellion, the federal government had the right to interfere with the property rights of slave owners, which had previously been considered sacrosanct. And, in practice, the confiscation policies of the Lincoln Administration allowed individual military commanders to provide de facto freedom to slaves who had been employed by the Confederate military and who reached Union lines. The President also took steps to promote his long-held goal of gradual abolition at the state level. In November 1861, he met with a pair of representatives from Delaware (a slave state that had rejected secession) to suggest that the state initiate gradual emancipation with compensation for slave owners. A month later, Lincoln asked the Congress to appropriate money to fund the voluntary emigration out of the country of any slaves that might be freed by state action. The following March, Lincoln urged Congress to approve funds to provide financial compensation to slave owners in any state that chose to abolish slavery. The President also began to directly lobby leaders of the border slave states (slave states that had rejected secession) in favor of gradual emancipation. Finally, in April, Lincoln signed legislation for gradual abolition in the District of Columbia, with financial compensation for those who could demonstrate their loyalty to the Union.

Although by the standards of the Emancipation Proclamation (1863) and the Thirteenth Amendment (which abolished slavery throughout the United States in 1865), Lincoln's initial steps against the institution of slavery seem modest and half-hearted, when measured against previous US history, they were truly unprecedented. Never before had the power of the federal government been used to free slaves from bondage. Nor had a president proposed that the financial resources of the federal government be used to promote emancipation within states where it was legal; and no president had ever personally lobbied leaders within individual states to adopt emancipation legislation. The steps that Lincoln took during the first year of the war were fully consistent with his longstanding belief in gradual, voluntary, and compensated emancipation. The vigor with which he pursued these steps (even in the midst of a bloody war) demonstrated his commitment to that goal.

---

5   Lincoln to William H. Seward, February 1, 1861, in *The Collected Works of Abraham Lincoln*, ed. Roy P. Basler, vol. 4 (New Brunswick, NJ: Rutgers University Press, 1953), 183.

The stubborn refusal of the slaveholding border states to cooperate with gradual emancipation, however, undermined Lincoln's efforts. On July 12, 1862, the president met with border state congressional representatives in a final effort to promote his gradual abolition plans, but to little avail. Meanwhile, congressional Republicans were taking increasingly bold action against slavery. In March, Congress passed legislation barring the army from returning fugitive slaves, regardless of circumstances. In July, just days after the President's unsuccessful attempt to lobby the border state representatives, Congress passed the Second Confiscation Act, which declared all slaves free who came within Union lines and whose owners were disloyal. Lincoln thus stood as a crossroads. He could continue to promote gradual emancipation—despite the fact that his efforts to do so had been largely stymied. Or he could accept the conclusion that many in his party had already come to—that the time had arrived to end slavery by direct federal action. While we may never know with certainty what was in Lincoln's mind in that pivotal month of July 1862, much is certain. Lincoln had a deep moral opposition to slavery. He had long opposed immediate emancipation through direct federal action for fear of the revolutionary turmoil and strife that such a step would provoke. By July of 1862, however, the path to gradual emancipation was blocked; and the nation was already embroiled in a destructive civil war. In these circumstances, Lincoln's moral principles required him to take direct action against slavery. The result was his decision to issue the Emancipation Proclamation, which he announced to his cabinet on July 21, 1862.

The destruction of slavery was not the work of any one person. Abolitionists, many of them inspired by former slaves, had struggled for decades to raise the moral consciousness of a nation. Thousands of enslaved African Americans took the opportunities offered by the Civil War to grasp for freedom. Anti-slavery legislators like Lyman Trumbull and Thaddeus Stevens pushed a cautious president to be bolder and braver by shepherding confiscation legislation through the Congress. During that fateful month of July 1862, however, the future of slavery truly did rest in the hands of one man. And in that moment, Abraham Lincoln, guided by his moral principles, took a step that would forever change the course of American history. For this reason, Lincoln does deserve the title of the "Great Emancipator."

POSITION #3—"DECISIVE AND EXTREME MEASURES MUST BE ADOPTED"

Emancipation and Total War

In Abraham Lincoln's famed August 1862 letter to newspaper editor Horace Greeley, the President declared the preservation of the Union to be his paramount object in the bloody war that was now in its second year. "What I do about slavery, and the colored race, I do because I believe it helps to save the Union," wrote Lincoln; "and what I forbear, I forbear because I do not believe it would help to save the Union."[11] Historians have long understood that Lincoln's letter to Greeley cannot be taken on face value. A month earlier, the President had decided to issue a general emancipation proclamation, and he was waiting for the proper moment to announce his decision. Lincoln's letter to Greeley must thus be understood as part of a campaign to prepare the northern public, much of which was lukewarm at best toward emancipation, for the bold step that was soon to come.

It would nonetheless be difficult to find a more clear and precise summary of the factors that led to Lincoln's decision for emancipation than that found in the Greeley letter. Lincoln did have a longstanding moral opposition to the institution of slavery. His moral critique of slavery, though, was tempered by his fear for the social and political turmoil that would result from the rapid elimination of the institution. Lincoln also doubted the ability of black and white Americans to live together on terms of equality should slavery be abolished. For these reasons, Lincoln had long favored gradual and voluntary abolition and had encouraged black emigration from the United States. With the eruption of hostilities and war in 1861, Lincoln sought to restrain the war's disruptive impact on the institution of slavery in the hopes that the rebellion could be rapidly suppressed with a minimum of bloodshed. The failure of General George B. McClellan's Peninsula Campaign in the spring and early summer of 1862, however, forced the President to rethink his position. Faced with the prospect of a long and bloody war in which victory was far from certain, Lincoln reluctantly accepted that the Civil War would become what historians call a "total war"—a war in which one must marshal all of one's resources to wear down and ultimately destroy the enemy's ability to fight. Lincoln's decision to issue the Emancipation Proclamation reflected his conclusion that the Union could only be preserved taking direct

---

11   Lincoln to Horace Greeley, August 22, 1863, in *The Collected Works of Abraham Lincoln*, ed. Roy P. Basler, vol. 5 (New Brunswick, NJ: Rutgers University Press, 1953), 388–389.

aim at the institution of slavery and by enlisting the enslaved as allies in the cause. As historian Glenn David Brasher argues, for Lincoln, emancipation was a crucial "lever" for winning the war.[12]

In his March 1861 inaugural address, President Lincoln set forth the policies that would guide him through the first year of the war. The Union, he proclaimed, was indivisible, and secession was therefore an act of insurrection. As president, he was constitutionally required to ensure the faithful execution of the laws throughout the nation, but he insisted that in doing so he would employ the minimum level of force required. The southern states, he maintained, would not be subject to an armed invasion and occupation unless the rebels themselves forced his hand. Lincoln also took the opportunity to reassure southern slave owners that he had neither the intention, the desire, nor the authority to interfere with the institution of slavery within states where it already existed, a position that he had maintained throughout his career in public life.[13] In providing these assurances, Lincoln hoped to limit the spread of secessionist sentiment and maintain the loyalty of as many southerners as possible. Lincoln also hoped to keep a northern public divided along party lines (and one in which advocates of abolition were a distinct minority) united in the cause of preserving the Union.

Even after the Confederate attack on Fort Sumter, Lincoln worked to keep the conflict limited. His initial April 1861 call for troops was for just 75,000 state militiamen who would enter into federal service for ninety days to suppress the rebellion. A few weeks later, he issued a call for 42,000 three-year volunteers and authorized an approximate doubling of size of the country's small regular army. (At the outbreak of hostilities, just 16,000 men were enlisted in the US Army.) Only in July, once the scope of the rebellion was clear, did Lincoln seek congressional approval to raise large numbers of troops. Lincoln also continued to insist that his sole purpose in the conflict was to preserve the Union and to ensure compliance with the law. In this effort, he had the support of the Congress, which in July approved a resolution stating that it was the disunionists of the southern states that had forced the conflict on the country. The resolution's key passage read, "This war is not prosecuted upon our part in any spirit of oppression, nor for any purpose of conquest or subjugation, nor purpose of overthrowing or interfering with the rights or established institutions of those States, but to defend and maintain the supremacy of the Constitution."[14]

In the first year of the war, Lincoln resisted growing pressure to strike broadly against the institution of slavery. While he approved the confiscation of slaves employed in support of the rebellion and lobbied the border states for gradual emancipation, he continued to assure southern slave owners that if the Confederates simply lay down their arms and affirmed their loyalty to the United States, the Union as it was (with slavery intact) could be restored. In September 1861, he rescinded a proclamation from John C. Frémont, the federal military commander in Missouri, that had declared all slaves in the state owned by rebel

---

12 Glenn David Brasher, *The Peninsula Campaign and the Necessity of Emancipation: African Americans and the Fight for Freedom* (Chapel Hill: University of North Carolina Press, 2012), 204.

13 Lincoln, "First Inaugural Address," March 4, 1861, in *The Collected Works of Abraham Lincoln*, ed. Roy P. Basler, vol. 4 (New Brunswick, NJ: Rutgers University Press, 1953), 262–271.

14 *Journal of the Senate*, 37th Cong., July 25, 1861, 1st Sess., 92.

sympathizers to be free. Lincoln's concern that the conflict not escalate in the direction of total war was apparent in his December 1861 annual message to Congress. "In considering the policy to be adopted for suppressing the insurrection, I have been anxious and careful that the inevitable conflict for this purpose shall not degenerate into a violent and remorseless revolutionary struggle," wrote Lincoln. "The Union must be preserved, and hence, all indispensable means must be employed. We should not be in haste to determine that radical and extreme measures, which may reach the loyal as well as the disloyal, are indispensable."[15] In May 1862, he overturned an order from General David Hunter declaring all slaves in South Carolina, Georgia, and Florida to be free. Over a year into the conflict, Lincoln still held hope that the rebellion could be suppressed by conventional military means. Moreover, by taking a moderate path, he maintained popular support for the war in the North and avoided provoking border states from joining the secession movement.

The President's hopes were dashed, however, by the failure of General George B. McClellan's Peninsula Campaign in the spring and early summer of 1862. In March 1862, 70,000 federal troops under McClellan's command landed at Fort Monroe in coastal Virginia and began gradually working their way toward the Confederate capital of Richmond. By late

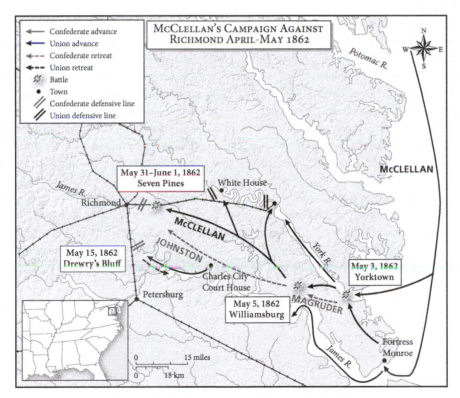

MAP 2. MCCLELLAN'S CAMPAIGN AGAINST RICHMOND APRIL–MAY 1862

---

15 Lincoln, "Annual Message to Congress," December 3, 1861, in *The Collected Works of Abraham Lincoln*, ed. Roy P. Basler, vol. 5 (New Brunswick, NJ: Rutgers University Press, 1953), 48–49.

May, McClellan had reached the outskirts of the city, but there found himself stymied. A late June Confederate counterattack brought McClellan's campaign, as well as northern expectations of rapid and easy military victory, to an end. (See Map 2, "McClellan's Campaign Against Richmond, April-May 1862.")

In the wake of McClellan's defeat, voices across the North increased their calls for more forceful measures against the Confederacy, including direct action against the institution of slavery. The Peninsula Campaign revealed the importance of slave labor, which had been employed with good effect by the Confederate military, to the rebel war effort. At the same time, the growing number of fugitive slaves that escaped to Union lines demonstrated that if given the proper incentive, large numbers of enslaved laborers would abandon the Confederacy and become a potential source of support for the Union. In early July, President Lincoln visited McClellan at his camp in coastal Virginia to evaluate the military situation for himself. In a letter that the General handed to the President, McClellan pushed back hard against those who advocated an escalation of the war. The conflict, he wrote, "should not be, at all, a War upon population; but against armed forces and political organizations . . . Military power should not be allowed to interfere with the relations of servitude, either by supporting or impairing the authority of the master."[16]

Lincoln returned to Washington unconvinced. On July 13, he shared his intention to issue a general proclamation of emancipation with Secretary of War William H. Seward and Secretary of the Navy Gideon Welles, two of his trusted advisors. As Wells later recalled, the President expressed his reluctance to take such a step but had concluded that it was unavoidable. The war could not be won, explained Lincoln, by a "temporizing and forbearing policy." Instead, "decisive and extreme measures" were necessary.[17] Meanwhile, in mid July, the Congress approved a sweeping confiscation act that freed all slaves that came within federal lines whose owners were in support of the Confederacy. The act also authorized the President to employ former slaves in any capacity he deemed necessary to suppress the rebellion. While there remained pockets of intense resistance to the idea of emancipation, most northerners by then perceived that slavery had been the root cause of the war and were therefore ready to wage war against slavery to preserve the Union—and they were ready to enlist black men as allies in that cause. On July 22, the President presented his decision to the full cabinet as one of a number of measures that reflected a shift toward total war. At the suggestion of his cabinet members, Lincoln agreed to delay the issuing of the proclamation until a more favorable moment in the military struggle.

In an August 1864 letter to a Wisconsin newspaper editor, President Lincoln explained that the intent of the Emancipation Proclamation was to induce African American people to "come bodily over from the rebel side to ours."[18] The results of the Emancipation

---

16 George B. McClellan to Abraham Lincoln, July 7, 1862, in *The War of the Rebellion: A Compilation of the Official Records of the Union and Confederate Armies*, Series 1, vol. 11, pt. 1, 73–74.

17 Gideon Welles, "The History of Emancipation," *The Galaxy* 14 (December 1872), 842.

18 Lincoln to Charles D. Robinson, August 17, 1864, in *The Collected Works of Abraham Lincoln*, ed. Roy P. Basler, vol. 7 (New Brunswick, NJ: Rutgers University Press, 1953), 499–501.

Proclamation were exactly as Lincoln intended. By 1865, roughly 200,000 black men (the majority of them former slaves) had enrolled in the United States military; and by the end of the war, black soldiers comprised about 15% of Union army. Thousands more provided support to the war as civilian military laborers and by providing intelligence to the Union army as it pressed south. The southern economy also suffered a significant loss of labor through the mass escape of slaves to Union lines as well as through acts of day-to-day resistance from enslaved workers emboldened by the prospect of freedom. In the end, decisive and extreme measures were indeed required to suppress the rebellion. That Lincoln adopted such measures, reluctantly and in violation of his long-held political principles, marks his greatness as a wartime leader.

DEBATING THE QUESTION

LINCOLN AND SLAVERY

Abraham Lincoln was an intensely private man who rarely shared his innermost thoughts and feelings with others. In addition, there is little documentation of his early life. His personal views on slavery must therefore be pieced together from his public statements and a handful of private writings in which he addresses the subject.

1.1 DAN STONE AND ABRAHAM LINCOLN, "PROTEST IN ILLINOIS LEGISLATURE ON SLAVERY" (1837)

Prior to the 1850s, Lincoln rarely commented publicly on the issue of slavery. One of his earliest public statements on slavery came while a twenty-eight-year-old member of the Illinois State Legislature. At the request of group of southern political leaders, the Illinois legislature had adopted three resolutions on the subject of slavery. The first condemned abolitionism; the second affirmed the constitutional right to own slaves in states where it was legal; and the third opposed efforts to abolish slavery in the District of Columbia, which was under the jurisdiction of the US Congress. After failing in an effort to amend the third resolution to include the words "unless the people of the said District petition for the same," Lincoln voted against all three resolutions, one of just six legislators to do so. Six weeks later, Lincoln and fellow legislator Dan Stone presented a formal protest in which they explained their votes against the resolutions.

GUIDING QUESTIONS:

1. What view does Lincoln take on the institution of slavery itself in this document?
2. What view does he take on abolitionism?
3. What powers does he say the federal government has to combat the institution of slavery?

PROTEST IN ILLINOIS LEGISLATURE ON SLAVERY

MARCH 3, 1837

The following protest was presented to the House, which was read and ordered to be spread on the journals, to wit:

"Resolutions upon the subject of domestic slavery having passed both branches of the General Assembly at its present session, the undersigned hereby protest against the passage of the same.

They believe that the institution of slavery is founded on both injustice and bad policy; but that the promulgation of abolition doctrines tends rather to increase than to abate its evils.

They believe that the Congress of the United States has no power, under the constitution, to interfere with the institution of slavery in the different States.

They believe that the Congress of the United States has the power, under the constitution, to abolish slavery in the District of Columbia; but that that power ought not to be exercised unless at the request of the people of said District.

The difference between these opinions and those contained in the said resolutions, is their reason for entering this protest."

DAN STONE,
A. LINCOLN,
Representatives from the county of Sangamon.

DRAWING CONCLUSIONS:

1. What can we learn from this document about a young Abraham Lincoln's position on the issue of slavery?

Roy P. Basler, ed., *The Collected Works of Abraham Lincoln*, vol. 1 (New Brunswick, NJ: Rutgers University Press, 1953), 74–75.

1.2 ABRAHAM LINCOLN TO MARY SPEED (1841)

The earliest existing documentation of Lincoln's private views on slavery come in this letter that a thirty-two-year-old Lincoln wrote to Mary Speed, the half sister of Lincoln's good friend Joshua Speed. The Speeds were a slave-owning Kentucky family. As a young man, Lincoln spent considerable time as a guest at the family's plantation near the city of Louisville. In the letter, Lincoln provides an account of a steamboat trip that he and Joshua Speed took from Louisville to St. Louis, Missouri, and he includes a brief description of a group of slaves who were on board the boat.

GUIDING QUESTIONS:

1. How does Lincoln describe the enslaved individuals he encountered on his trip?
2. What clues does this description provide about Lincoln's feelings on slavery?

LINCOLN TO MARY SPEED

MISS MARY SPEED, BLOOMINGTON, ILLINOIS,

LOUISVILLE, KY. SEPT. 27TH. 1841

My Friend: Having resolved to write to some of your mother's family, and not having the express permission of any one of them [to] do so, I have had some little difficulty in determining on which to inflict the task of reading what I now feel must be a most dull and silly letter; but when I remembered that you and I were something of cronies while I was at Farmington, and that, while there, I once was under the necessity of shutting you up in a room to prevent your committing an assault and battery upon me, I instantly decided that you should be the devoted one.

I assume that you have not heard from Joshua & myself since we left, because I think it doubtful whether he has written.

You remember there was some uneasiness about Joshua's health when we left. That little indisposition of his turned out to be nothing serious; and it was pretty nearly forgotten when we reached Springfield. We got on board the Steam Boat Lebanon, in the locks of the Canal about 12 o'clock. M. of the day we left, and reached St. Louis the next monday at 8 P.M.

Nothing of interest happened during the passage, except the vexatious delays occasioned by the sand bars be thought interesting. By the way, a fine example was presented on board the boat for contemplating the effect of condition upon human happiness. A gentleman had purchased twelve negroes in different parts of Kentucky and was taking them to a farm in the South. They were chained six and six together. A small iron clevis was around the left wrist of each, and this fastened to the main chain by a shorter one at a convenient distance from, the others; so that the negroes were strung together precisely like so many fish upon a trot-line. In this condition they were being separated forever from the scenes of their childhood, their friends, their fathers and mothers, and brothers and sisters, and many of them, from their wives and children, and going into perpetual slavery where the lash of the master is proverbially more ruthless and unrelenting than any other where; and yet amid all these distressing circumstances, as we would think them, they were the most cheerful and apparently happy creatures on board. One, whose offence for which he had been sold was an over-fondness for his wife, played the fiddle almost continually; and the others danced, sung, cracked jokes, and played various games with cards from day to day. How true it is

From Roy P. Basler, ed., *The Collected Works of Abraham Lincoln*, vol. 1 (New Brunswick, NJ: Rutgers University Press, 1953), 259–261.

that "God tempers the wind to the shorn lamb," or in other words, that He renders the worst of human conditions tolerable, while He permits the best, to be nothing better than tolerable.

To return to the narrative. When we reached Springfield, I staid but one day when I started on this tedious circuit where I now am. Do you remember my going to the city while I was in Kentucky, to have a tooth extracted, and making a failure of it? Well, that same old tooth got to paining me so much, that about a week since I had it torn out, bringing with it a bit of the jawbone; the consequence of which is that my mouth is now so sore that I can neither talk, nor eat. I am litterally "subsisting on savoury remembrances"—that is, being unable to eat, I am living upon the remembrance of the delicious dishes of peaches and cream we used to have at your house.

When we left, Miss Fanny Henning was owing you a visit, as I understood. Has she paid it yet? If she has, are you not convinced that she is one of the sweetest girls in the world? There is but one thing about her, so far as I could perceive, that I would have otherwise than as it is. That is something of a tendency to melancholly. This, let it be observed, is a misfortune not a fault. Give her an assurance of my verry highest regard, when you see her.

Is little Siss Eliza Davis at your house yet? If she is kiss her "o'er and o'er again" for me.

Tell your mother that I have not got her "present" with me; but that I intend to read it regularly when I return home. I doubt not that it is really, as she says, the best cure for the "Blues" could one but take it according to the truth.

Give my respects to all your sisters (including "Aunt Emma") and brothers. Tell Mrs. Peay, of whose happy face I shall long retain a pleasant remembrance, that I have been trying to think of a name for her homestead, but as yet, can not satisfy myself with one. I shall be verry happy to receive a line from you, soon after you receive this; and, in case you choose to favour me with one, address it to Charleston, Coles Co. Ills as I shall be there about the time to receive it. Your sincere friend A. LINCOLN

DRAWING CONCLUSIONS:

1. What can we learn from this document about a young Abraham Lincoln's personal feelings about slavery?

1.3 ABRAHAM LINCOLN, "SPEECH AT PEORIA, ILLINOIS" (1854)

After serving one term in the US Congress (1847–1849), Lincoln retired from public life and devoted himself to his law practice. He re-entered politics in 1854, however, in response to the passage of the Kansas-Nebraska Act, a law that allowed slavery in the newly organized territories of Kansas and Nebraska, where it had been previously banned. The Kansas-Nebraska Act aroused enormous controversy and opposition throughout the North, as it overturned the Missouri Compromise of 1820, a federal law that had excluded slavery from much of the nation's western territories. (The term "territory" referred to federal lands that had not yet been organized into states.) This document includes excerpts from a speech that Lincoln delivered in Peoria, Illinois, in 1854 at a joint appearance with US Senator Stephen Douglas ("Judge Douglas" in the document), the architect and leading advocate of the Kansas-Nebraska Act.

GUIDING QUESTIONS:

1. In this speech, what reasons does Lincoln give for opposing the expansion of slavery into the western territories?
2. What does Lincoln say should be done about the institution of slavery where it currently exists?
3. What views does Lincoln express in this speech on issues of race and racial equality?
4. What is his response to those who say that the opponents of slavery's expansion are threatening the Union?

SPEECH AT PEORIA, ILLINOIS

OCTOBER 16, 1854

MR. LINCOLN'S SPEECH.

The repeal of the Missouri Compromise, and the propriety of its restoration, constitute the subject of what I am about to say.

As I desire to present my own connected view of this subject, my remarks will not be, specifically, an answer to Judge Douglas; yet, as I proceed, the main points he has presented will arise, and will receive such respectful attention as I may be able to give them.

I wish further to say, that I do not propose to question the patriotism, or to assail the motives of any man, or class of men; but rather to strictly confine myself to the naked merits of the question.

I also wish to be no less than National in all the positions I may take; and whenever I take ground which others have thought, or may think, narrow, sectional and dangerous to the Union, I hope to give a reason, which will appear sufficient, at least to some, why I think differently.

And, as this subject is no other, than part and parcel of the larger general question of domestic-slavery, I wish to MAKE and to KEEP the distinction between the EXISTING institution, and the EXTENSION of it, so broad, and so clear, that no honest man can misunderstand me, and no dishonest one, successfully misrepresent me. . . .

From Roy P. Basler, ed., *The Collected Works of Abraham Lincoln*, vol. 2 (New Brunswick, NJ: Rutgers University Press, 1953), 247–271.

During this long period of time Nebraska had remained, substantially an uninhabited country, but now emigration to, and settlement within it began to take place. It is about one third as large as the present United States, and its importance so long overlooked, begins to come into view. The restriction of slavery by the Missouri Compromise directly applies to it; in fact, was first made, and has since been maintained, expressly for it. In 1853, a bill to give it a territorial government passed the House of Representatives, and, in the hands of Judge Douglas, failed of passing the Senate only for want of time. This bill contained no repeal of the Missouri Compromise. Indeed, when it was assailed because it did not contain such repeal, Judge Douglas defended it in its existing form. On January 4th, 1854, Judge Douglas introduces a new bill to give Nebraska territorial government. He accompanies this bill with a report, in which last, he expressly recommends that the Missouri Compromise shall neither be affirmed nor repealed.

Before long the bill is so modified as to make two territories instead of one; calling the Southern one Kansas.

Also, about a month after the introduction of the bill, on the judge's own motion, it is so amended as to declare the Missouri Compromise inoperative and void; and, substantially, that the People who go and settle there may establish slavery, or exclude it, as they may see fit. In this shape the bill passed both branches of congress, and became a law.

This is the repeal of the Missouri Compromise. The foregoing history may not be precisely accurate in every particular; but I am sure it is sufficiently so, for all the uses I shall attempt to make of it, and in it, we have before us, the chief material enabling us to correctly judge whether the repeal of the Missouri Compromise is right or wrong.

I think, and shall try to show, that it is wrong; wrong in its direct effect, letting slavery into Kansas and Nebraska—and wrong in its prospective principle, allowing it to spread to every other part of the wide world, where men can be found inclined to take it.

This declared indifference, but as I must think, covert real zeal for the spread of slavery, I can not

but hate. I hate it because of the monstrous injustice of slavery itself. I hate it because it deprives our republican example of its just influence in the world—enables the enemies of free institutions, with plausibility, to taunt us as hypocrites—causes the real friends of freedom to doubt our sincerity, and especially because it forces so many really good men amongst ourselves into an open war with the very fundamental principles of civil liberty—criticising the Declaration of Independence, and insisting that there is no right principle of action but self-interest.

Before proceeding, let me say I think I have no prejudice against the Southern people. They are just what we would be in their situation. If slavery did not now exist amongst them, they would not introduce it. If it did now exist amongst us, we should not instantly give it up. This I believe of the masses north and south. Doubtless there are individuals, on both sides, who would not hold slaves under any circumstances; and others who would gladly introduce slavery anew, if it were out of existence. We know that some southern men do free their slaves, go north, and become tip-top abolitionists; while some northern ones go south, and become most cruel slave-masters.

When southern people tell us they are no more responsible for the origin of slavery, than we; I acknowledge the fact. When it is said that the institution exists; and that it is very difficult to get rid of it, in any satisfactory way, I can understand and appreciate the saying. I surely will not blame them for not doing what I should not know how to do myself. If all earthly power were given me, I should not know what to do, as to the existing institution. My first impulse would be to free all the slaves, and send them to Liberia—to their own native land. But a moment's reflection would convince me, that whatever of high hope, (as I think there is) there may be in this, in the long run, its sudden execution is impossible. If they were all landed there in a day, they would all perish in the next ten days; and there are not surplus shipping and surplus money enough in the world to carry them there in many times ten days. What then? Free them all, and keep them among us as underlings? Is it quite certain that this betters their condition? I think

I would not hold one in slavery, at any rate; yet the point is not clear enough for me to denounce people upon. What next? Free them, and make them politically and socially, our equals? My own feelings will not admit of this; and if mine would, we well know that those of the great mass of white people will not. Whether this feeling accords with justice and sound judgment, is not the sole question, if indeed, it is any part of it. A universal feeling, whether well or ill-founded, can not be safely disregarded. We can not, then, make them equals. It does seem to me that systems of gradual emancipation might be adopted; but for their tardiness in this, I will not undertake to judge our brethren of the south.

When they remind us of their constitutional rights, I acknowledge them, not grudgingly, but fully, and fairly; and I would give them any legislation for the reclaiming of their fugitives, which should not, in its stringency, be more likely to carry a free man into slavery, than our ordinary criminal laws are to hang an innocent one.

But all this; to my judgment, furnishes no more excuse for permitting slavery to go into our own free territory, than it would for reviving the African slave trade by law. The law which forbids the bringing of slaves from Africa; and that which has so long forbid the taking them to Nebraska, can hardly be distinguished on any moral principle; and the repeal of the former could find quite as plausible excuses as that of the latter. . . .

But Nebraska is urged as a great Union-saving measure. Well I too, go for saving the Union. Much as I hate slavery, I would consent to the extension of it rather than see the Union dissolved, just as I would consent to any GREAT evil, to avoid a GREATER one. But when I go to Union saving, I must believe, at least, that the means I employ has some adaptation to the end. To my mind, Nebraska has no such adaptation.

"It hath no relish of salvation in it."

It is an aggravation, rather, of the only one thing which ever endangers the Union. When it came upon us, all was peace and quiet. The nation was looking to the forming of new bonds of Union; and a long course of peace and prosperity seemed to lie before us. In the whole range of possibility, there scarcely appears to me to have been any thing, out of which the slavery agitation could have been revived, except the very project of repealing the Missouri compromise. Every inch of territory we owned, already had a definite settlement of the slavery question, and by which, all parties were pledged to abide. Indeed, there was no uninhabited country on the continent, which we could acquire; if we except some extreme northern regions, which are wholly out of the question. In this state of case, the genius of Discord himself, could scarcely have invented a way of again getting us by the ears, but by turning back and destroying the peace measures of the past. The councils of that genius seem to have prevailed, the Missouri compromise was repealed; and here we are, in the midst of a new slavery agitation, such, I think, as we have never seen before.

Who is responsible for this? Is it those who resist the measure; or those who, causelessly, brought it forward, and pressed it through, having reason to know, and, in fact, knowing it must and would be so resisted? It could not but be expected by its author, that it would be looked upon as a measure for the extension of slavery, aggravated by a gross breach of faith. Argue as you will, and long as you will, this is the naked FRONT and ASPECT, of the measure. And in this aspect, it could not but produce agitation. Slavery is founded in the selfishness of man's nature—opposition to it, is [in?] his love of justice. These principles are an eternal antagonism; and when brought into collision so fiercely, as slavery extension brings them, shocks, and throes, and convulsions must ceaselessly follow. Repeal the Missouri compromise—repeal all compromises—repeal the declaration of independence—repeal all past history, you still can not repeal human nature. It still will be the abundance of man's heart, that slavery extension is wrong; and out of the abundance of his heart, his mouth will continue to speak. . . .

DRAWING CONCLUSIONS:

1. What can we learn from this document about Abraham Lincoln's position on the issues of slavery and race in the 1850s?

1.4   ABRAHAM LINCOLN
TO JOSHUA F. SPEED (1855)

Following the passage of the Kansas-Nebraska Act, the issue of slavery's expansion into the western territories came to increasingly dominate national politics. It also began to fray the friendship between Lincoln and his longtime friend, Joshua Speed, a Kentucky slaveowner. In 1855, Lincoln wrote a long private letter to Speed in which he explained his views on slavery in depth in hopes that the two men's friendship might survive their political disagreement. This letter offers among the most detailed windows into Lincoln's private thoughts on the slavery question. In these short excerpts, Lincoln summarizes his overall views on the subject. Note that he refers to the 1841 steamboat trip with Speed that Lincoln had earlier described to Speed's half sister Mary in his 1841 letter. He also makes reference to "Know Nothings," a nickname for the "American Party," an anti-immigrant, anti-Catholic political party that briefly rose to prominence in the mid 1850s.

GUIDING QUESTIONS:

1. How, in this letter, does Lincoln say he *feels* about slavery?
2. Why, according to Lincoln, does he not act on his feelings by advocating for the abolition of slavery?

LINCOLN TO JOSHUA F. SPEED

SPRINGFIELD, AUG. 24, 1855

Dear Speed:
    You know what a poor correspondent I am. Ever since I received your very agreeable letter of the 22nd. of May I have been intending to write you in answer to it. You suggest that in political action now, you and I would differ. I suppose we would; not quite as much, however, as you may think. You know I dislike slavery; and you fully admit the abstract wrong of it. So far there is no cause of difference. But you say that sooner than yield your legal right to the slave—especially at the bidding of those who are not themselves interested, you would see the Union dissolved. I am not aware that any one is bidding you to yield that right; very certainly I am not. I leave that matter entirely to yourself. I also acknowledge your rights and my obligations, under the constitution, in regard to your slaves. I confess I hate to see the poor creatures hunted down, and caught, and carried back to their stripes, and unrewarded toils; but I bite my lip and keep quiet. In 1841 you and I had together a tedious low-water trip, on a Steam Boat from Louisville to St. Louis. You may remember, as I well do, that from Louisville to the mouth of the Ohio there were, on board, ten or a dozen slaves, shackled together with irons. That sight was a continual torment to me; and I see something like it every time I touch the Ohio, or any other slave-border. It is hardly fair for you to assume, that I have no interest in a thing which has, and continually exercises, the power of making me miserable. You ought rather to appreciate how much the great body of the Northern people do crucify their feelings, in order to maintain their loyalty to the constitution and the Union.

I do oppose the extension of slavery, because my judgment and feelings so prompt me; and I am under

From Roy P. Basler, ed., *The Collected Works of Abraham Lincoln*, vol. 2 (New Brunswick, NJ: Rutgers University Press, 1953), 320–323.

no obligation to the contrary. If for this you and I must differ, differ we must. . . .

I am not a Know-Nothing. That is certain. How could I be? How can any one who abhors the oppression of negroes, be in favor of degrading classes of white people? Our progress in degeneracy appears to me to be pretty rapid. As a nation, we began by declaring that "all men are created equal." We now practically read it "all men are created equal, except negroes." When the Know-Nothings get control, it will read "all men are created equal, except negroes, and foreigners, and catholics." When it comes to this I should prefer emigrating to some country where they make no pretence of loving liberty—to Russia, for instance, where despotism can be taken pure, and without the base alloy of hypocracy.

Mary will probably pass a day or two in Louisville in October. My kindest regards to Mrs. Speed. On the leading subject of this letter, I have more of her sympathy than I have of yours.

And yet let [me] say I am Your friend forever
A. LINCOLN—

DRAWING CONCLUSIONS:

1. What can we learn from this document about Lincoln's private feelings about slavery and their influence on his public position on the issue? Do his views seem to have evolved since his 1841 letter to Mary Speed?

1.5   ABRAHAM LINCOLN, "FRAGMENT AGAINST SLAVERY" (1858)

By 1858, Lincoln had emerged as the state of Illinois's leading opponent of the expansion of slavery into the western territories. In 1858, the recently established Republican Party (an anti-slavery party) nominated him as its candidate to challenge incumbent US Senator Stephen Douglas. Lincoln and Douglas agreed to a series of one-on-one candidate debates in communities throughout Illinois. This document is a brief private note that Lincoln wrote to himself in the context of the Lincoln–Douglas debates. In the note, Lincoln compares his Senate candidacy to the struggles of British politician William Wilberforce and reformer Granville Sharp to end the British slave trade. Lincoln's reason for drafting this note is unknown.

GUIDING QUESTIONS:

1. In this note, what does Lincoln say are his motives in his Senate campaign?
2. In what ways does he say his efforts are similar to those of Wilberforce and Sharp?

LINCOLN, FRAGMENT ON THE STRUGGLE AGAINST SLAVERY

[c. JULY 1858]

I have never professed an indifference to the honors of official station; and were I to do so now, I should only make myself ridiculous. Yet I have never failed—do not now fail—to remember that in the republican cause there is a higher aim than that of mere office. I have not allowed myself to forget that the abolition of the Slave-trade by Great Brittain, was agitated a hundred years before it was a final success; that the measure had it's open fire-eating opponents; it's stealthy "don't care" opponents; it's dollar and cent opponents; it's inferior race opponents; its negro equality opponents; and its religion and good order opponents; that all these opponents got offices, and their adversaries got none. But I have also remembered that though they blazed, like tallow-candles for a century, at last they flickered in the socket, died out, stank in the dark for a brief season, and were remembered no more, even by the smell. School-boys know that Wilbe[r]force, and Granville Sharpe [*sic*], helped that cause forward; but who can now name a single man who labored to retard it? Remembering these things I can not but regard it as possible that the higher object of this contest may not be completely attained within the term of my natural life. But I can not doubt either that it will come in due time. Even in this view, I am proud, in my passing speck of time, to contribute an humble mite to that glorious consummation, which my own poor eyes may not last to see.

DRAWING CONCLUSIONS:

1. What does this document suggest about Lincoln's political motives in the 1850s?

From Roy P. Basler, ed., *The Collected Works of Abraham Lincoln*, vol. 2 (New Brunswick, NJ: Rutgers University Press, 1953), 482.

SLAVERY AND THE SECESSION CRISIS

Abraham Lincoln was elected President on November 6, 1860, and took office in March of the following year. (In the nineteenth century, the presidential inauguration took place on March 4 of the year following the election.) Within days of Lincoln's election, political leaders in a number of southern states took steps to initiate the process of secession from the United States of America. Much of President-elect Lincoln's energy between November and March was devoted to the issue of secession, including efforts to resolve the crisis through political compromise. Attempts to find a compromise solution ended in failure, and the result was armed conflict between southern rebels and the federal government.

2.1   ABRAHAM LINCOLN TO WILLIAM KELLOGG (DECEMBER 11, 1860)

One key issue in compromise talks was the extension of slavery into the western territories. Lincoln and Republican members of Congress, who had been elected on a promise to halt the expansion of slavery, faced enormous pressure to weaken their stance to preserve national unity. A second issue was enforcement of the fugitive slave clause of the United States Constitution. The Constitution required that those who escaped slavery by fleeing to free states be returned to their owners. Southern slave owners had long pressed for stringent enforcement of this requirement. In 1850, the US Congress enacted a controversial fugitive slave law that was opposed and actively resisted by many anti-slavery northerners. In this letter to Illinois Republican Congressman William Kellogg, Lincoln states his position on both of these key issues. (Lincoln wrote numerous similar letters to Republican officials and politicians during the secession crisis.) At the time of this letter, the secession process was well underway in a number of states, but no state had yet actually voted to secede from the Union.

GUIDING QUESTIONS:

1. At the time of this letter, what was Lincoln's position on the slavery extension issue? What reason does he give for taking this position?
2. At the time of this letter, what was Lincoln's position on the fugitive slave issue?

LINCOLN TO WILLIAM KELLOGG

PRIVATE & CONFIDENTIAL. HON. WILLIAM KELLOGG. SPRINGFIELD, ILLS.

DEC. 11. 1860

My dear Sir—
    Entertain no proposition for a compromise in regard to the extension of slavery. The instant you do, they have us under again; all our labor is lost, and sooner or later must be done over. Douglas is sure to be again trying to bring in his "Pop. Sov." Have none of it. The tug has to come & better now than later.

You know I think the fugitive slave clause of the constitution ought to be enforced—to put it on the mildest form, ought not to be resisted. In haste Yours as ever A. LINCOLN

DRAWING CONCLUSIONS:

1. What does this letter reveal about Lincoln's stance on the slavery issue in the early stages of the secession crisis? To what extent was he willing to compromise?
2. What does this letter reveal about Lincoln's reasons for taking this stance?

From Roy P. Basler, ed., *The Collected Works of Abraham Lincoln*, vol. 4 (New Brunswick, NJ: Rutgers University Press, 1953), 150.

2.2   ABRAHAM LINCOLN TO ALEXANDER STEPHENS (DECEMBER 22, 1860)

On December 20, 1860, a special statewide convention proclaimed South Carolina's independence from the United States. Two days later, Lincoln sent this letter to longtime friend and associate Alexander Stephens, a prominent Georgia politician who was opposed to secession. (Following Georgia's secession from the Union, Stephens declared his loyalty to the state and was elected Vice President of the Confederate States of America.) This letter was part of a systematic effort by Lincoln to persuade southern slave owners that their interests would be secure under his presidency.

GUIDING QUESTIONS:

1. What reassurances does Lincoln give southern slave owners in this letter?
2. What position does Lincoln take on the slavery question in this letter?

LINCOLN TO ALEXANDER H. STEPHENS

FOR YOUR OWN EYE ONLY. HON. A. H. STEPHENS—SPRINGFIELD, ILLS.

DEC. 22, 1860

My dear Sir

Your obliging answer to my short note is just received, and for which please accept my thanks. I fully appreciate the present peril the country is in, and the weight of responsibility on me.

Do the people of the South really entertain fears that a Republican administration would, directly, or indirectly, interfere with their slaves, or with them, about their slaves? If they do, I wish to assure you, as once a friend, and still, I hope, not an enemy, that there is no cause for such fears.

The South would be in no more danger in this respect, than it was in the days of Washington. I suppose, however, this does not meet the case. You think slavery is right and ought to be extended; while we think it is wrong and ought to be restricted. That I suppose is the rub. It certainly is the only substantial difference between us. Yours very truly A. LINCOLN

DRAWING CONCLUSIONS:

1. What does this letter reveal about Lincoln's position on slavery during the secession crisis?

From Roy P. Basler, ed., *The Collected Works of Abraham Lincoln*, vol. 4 (New Brunswick, NJ: Rutgers University Press, 1953), 160–161.

2.3 ABRAHAM LINCOLN TO JAMES T. HALE (JANUARY 11, 1861)

On January 6, 1861, Pennsylvania Republican Congressman James T. Hale wrote to Lincoln recommending a series of compromise measures to resolve the secession crisis. Hale's recommendations included a Constitutional amendment barring Congress from abolishing slavery in the states; a Congressional resolution declaring that slavery would not be abolished in the District of Columbia without the consent of both its residents and of the neighboring slave state of Maryland; a strengthening of the fugitive slave law; and the drawing of a line through the western territories north of which slavery would be barred and south of which it would be allowed. In this letter, Lincoln responds to Hale's proposals. The letter includes a detailed rationale for Lincoln's rejection of any compromise measure related to the expansion of slavery. In the letter, Lincoln references previous efforts to have the Caribbean Island of Cuba annexed to the United States as a slave territory.

GUIDING QUESTIONS:

1. What reasons does Lincoln give in this letter for rejecting compromise proposals on the issue of slavery expansion?

LINCOLN TO JAMES T. HALE

CONFIDENTIAL. HON. J. T. HALE SPRINGFIELD, ILL. JAN'Y. 11TH 1861.

My dear Sir—Yours of the 6th is received. I answer it only because I fear you would misconstrue my silence. What is our present condition? We have just carried an election on principles fairly stated to the people. Now we are told in advance, the government shall be broken up, unless we surrender to those we have beaten, before we take the offices. In this they are either attempting to play upon us, or they are in dead earnest. Either way, if we surrender, it is the end of us, and of the government. They will repeat the experiment upon us ad libitum. A year will not pass, till we shall have to take Cuba as a condition upon which they will stay in the Union. They now have the Constitution, under which we have lived over seventy years, and acts of Congress of their own framing, with no prospect of their being changed; and they can never have a more shallow pretext for breaking up the government, or extorting a compromise, than now. There is, in my judgment, but one compromise which would really settle the slavery question, and that would be a prohibition against acquiring any more territory. Yours very truly, A. LINCOLN.

DRAWING CONCLUSIONS:

1. What can we learn from this letter about the reasons for Lincoln's hard-line stance on the slavery expansion issue during the secession crisis?

From Roy P. Basler, ed., *The Collected Works of Abraham Lincoln*, vol. 4 (New Brunswick, NJ: Rutgers University Press, 1953), 172.

2.4 ABRAHAM LINCOLN TO WILLIAM H. SEWARD (FEBRUARY 1, 1861)

By February of 1861, seven southern states had seceded from the United States and begun the process of establishing the Confederate States of America. Meanwhile, in Washington, DC, political leaders continued to search for a compromise that would preserve the Union. Senator John J. Crittenden of Kentucky proposed a set of constitutional amendments, including one that would divide the western territories in half, with slavery allowed in the southern half but barred in the northern half. In this letter to William H. Seward, a prominent Republican whom Lincoln had selected for Secretary of State, Lincoln conveys his position on Crittenden's proposed compromise.

GUIDING QUESTIONS:

1. In this letter, on what issues does Lincoln express a willingness to compromise?
2. On what issues does Lincoln say he is unwilling to compromise? What reasons does he give for his hard-line stance on these issues?

LINCOLN TO WILLIAM H. SEWARD

PRIVATE & CONFIDENTIAL. HON. W. H. SEWARD SPRINGFIELD, ILLS. FEB. 1. 1861

My dear Sir On the 21st. ult. Hon. W. Kellogg, a Republican M.C of this state whom you probably know, was here, in a good deal of anxiety, seeking to ascertain to what extent I would be consenting for our friends to go in the way of compromise on the now vexed question. While he was with me I received a despatch from Senator Trumbull, at Washington, alluding to the same question, and telling me to await letters. I thereupon told Mr. Kellogg that when I should receive these letters, posting me as to the state of affairs at Washington, I would write you, requesting you to let him see my letter. To my surprise when the letters mentioned by Judge Trumbull came, they made no allusion to the "vexed question"[.] This baffled me so much that I was near not writing you at all, in compliance with what I had said to Judge Kellogg.

I say now, however, as I have all the while said, that on the territorial question—that is, the question of extending slavery under the national auspices,—I am inflexible. I am for no compromise which assists or permits the extension of the institution on soil owned by the nation. And any trick by which the nation is to acquire territory, and then allow some local authority to spread slavery over it, is as obnoxious as any other.

I take it that to effect some such result as this, and to put us again on the high-road to a slave empire is the object of all these proposed compromises. I am against it.

As to fugitive slaves, District of Columbia, slave trade among the slave states, and whatever springs of necessity from the fact that the institution is amongst us, I care but little, so that what is done be comely, and not altogether outrageous. Nor do I care much about New-Mexico, if further extension were hedged against. Yours very truly A. LINCOLN—

DRAWING CONCLUSIONS:

1. What does this letter reveal about Lincoln's stance on the slavery issue in the later stages of the secession crisis?
2. How, if at all, had Lincoln's position evolved since the early stages of the secession crisis?

From Roy P. Basler, ed., *The Collected Works of Abraham Lincoln*, vol. 4 (New Brunswick, NJ: Rutgers University Press, 1953), 183.

2.5 ABRAHAM LINCOLN, "FIRST INAUGURAL ADDRESS" (MARCH 4, 1861)

Lincoln took office as president on March 4, 1861. At that time, seven southern states had seceded and established the Confederate States of America. Another eight slave states, however, had so far rejected calls for secession. Lincoln devoted the entirety of his inaugural address to the issues of slavery and secession, setting forth his administration's position on both of these key issues. At the time that this speech was delivered, fighting between Confederate and Union forces had not yet commenced. Many still hoped for a peaceful resolution of the crisis.

GUIDING QUESTIONS:

1. What position on the issue of slavery does Lincoln take in his inaugural address?
2. What position on the issue of secession does Lincoln take in his inaugural address?
3. What reassurances does Lincoln provide southern slave owners in his inaugural address?

FIRST INAUGURAL ADDRESS—FINAL TEXT

MARCH 4, 1861

Fellow citizens of the United States:

In compliance with a custom as old as the government itself, I appear before you to address you briefly, and to take, in your presence, the oath prescribed by the Constitution of the United States, to be taken by the President "before he enters on the execution of his office."

I do not consider it necessary, at present, for me to discuss those matters of administration about which there is no special anxiety, or excitement.

Apprehension seems to exist among the people of the Southern States, that by the accession of a Republican Administration, their property, and their peace, and personal security, are to be endangered. There has never been any reasonable cause for such apprehension. Indeed, the most ample evidence to the contrary has all the while existed, and been open to their inspection. It is found in nearly all the published speeches of him who now addresses you.

I do but quote from one of those speeches when I declare that "I have no purpose, directly or indirectly, to interfere with the institution of slavery in the States where it exists. I believe I have no lawful right to do so, and I have no inclination to do so." Those who nominated and elected me did so with full knowledge that I had made this, and many similar declarations, and had never recanted them. And more than this, they placed in the platform, for my acceptance, and as a law to themselves, and to me, the clear and emphatic resolution which I now read:

"Resolved, That the maintenance inviolate of the rights of the States, and especially the right of each State to order and control its own domestic institutions according to its own judgment exclusively, is essential to that balance of power on which the perfection and endurance of our political fabric depend; and we denounce the lawless invasion by armed force of the soil of any State or Territory, no matter under what pretext, as among the gravest of crimes."

I now reiterate these sentiments: and in doing so, I only press upon the public attention the most conclusive evidence of which the case is susceptible, that

From Roy P. Basler, ed., *The Collected Works of Abraham Lincoln*, vol. 4 (New Brunswick, NJ: Rutgers University Press, 1953), 262–271.

the property, peace and security of no section are to be in anywise endangered by the now incoming Administration. I add too, that all the protection which, consistently with the Constitution and the laws, can be given, will be cheerfully given to all the States when lawfully demanded, for whatever cause—as cheerfully to one section, as to another.

There is much controversy about the delivering up of fugitives from service or labor. The clause I now read is as plainly written in the Constitution as any other of its provisions:

"No person held to service or labor in one State, under the laws thereof, escaping into another, shall, in consequence of any law or regulation therein, be discharged from such service or labor, but shall be delivered up on claim of the party to whom such service or labor may be due."

It is scarcely questioned that this provision was intended by those who made it, for the reclaiming of what we call fugitive slaves; and the intention of the law-giver is the law. All members of Congress swear their support to the whole Constitution—to this provision as much as to any other. To the proposition, then, that slaves whose cases come within the terms of this clause, "shall be delivered up," their oaths are unanimous. Now, if they would make the effort in good temper, could they not, with nearly equal unanimity, frame and pass a law, by means of which to keep good that unanimous oath?

There is some difference of opinion whether this clause should be enforced by national or by state authority; but surely that difference is not a very material one. If the slave is to be surrendered, it can be of but little consequence to him, or to others, by which authority it is done. And should any one, in any case, be content that his oath shall go unkept, on a merely unsubstantial controversy as to how it shall be kept?

Again, in any law upon this subject, ought not all the safeguards of liberty known in civilized and humane jurisprudence to be introduced, so that a free man be not, in any case, surrendered as a slave? And might it not be well, at the same time, to provide by law for the enforcement of that clause in the Constitution which guarranties that "The citizens of each State shall be entitled to all previleges and immunities of citizens in the several States?"

I take the official oath to-day, with no mental reservations, and with no purpose to construe the Constitution or laws, by any hypercritical rules. And while I do not choose now to specify particular acts of Congress as proper to be enforced, I do suggest, that it will be much safer for all, both in official and private stations, to conform to, and abide by, all those acts which stand unrepealed, than to violate any of them, trusting to find impunity in having them held to be unconstitutional.

It is seventy-two years since the first inauguration of a President under our national Constitution. During that period fifteen different and greatly distinguished citizens, have, in succession, administered the executive branch of the government. They have conducted it through many perils; and, generally, with great success. Yet, with all this scope for precedent, I now enter upon the same task for the brief constitutional term of four years, under great and peculiar difficulty. A disruption of the Federal Union heretofore only menaced, is now formidably attempted.

I hold, that in contemplation of universal law, and of the Constitution, the Union of these States is perpetual. Perpetuity is implied, if not expressed, in the fundamental law of all national governments. It is safe to assert that no government proper, ever had a provision in its organic law for its own termination. Continue to execute all the express provisions of our national Constitution, and the Union will endure forever—it being impossible to destroy it, except by some action not provided for in the instrument itself.

Again, if the United States be not a government proper, but an association of States in the nature of contract merely, can it, as a contract, be peaceably unmade, by less than all the parties who made it? One party to a contract may violate it—break it, so to speak; but does it not require all to lawfully rescind it?

Descending from these general principles, we find the proposition that, in legal contemplation, the Union is perpetual, confirmed by the history of the Union itself. The Union is much older than the Constitution. It was formed in fact, by the Articles of Association in 1774. It was matured and continued by the Declaration of Independence in 1776. It was further matured and the faith of all the then thirteen States expressly plighted and engaged that it should be perpetual, by the Articles of Confederation in 1778. And finally, in 1787, one of the declared objects for ordaining and establishing the Constitution, was "to form a more perfect union."

But if destruction of the Union, by one, or by a part only, of the States, be lawfully possible, the Union is less perfect than before the Constitution, having lost the vital element of perpetuity.

It follows from these views that no State, upon its own mere motion, can lawfully get out of the Union,—that resolves and ordinances to that effect are legally void; and that acts of violence, within any State or States, against the authority of the United States, are insurrectionary or revolutionary, according to circumstances.

I therefore consider that, in view of the Constitution and the laws, the Union is unbroken; and, to the extent of my ability, I shall take care, as the Constitution itself expressly enjoins upon me, that the laws of the Union be faithfully executed in all the States. Doing this I deem to be only a simple duty on my part; and I shall perform it, so far as practicable, unless my rightful masters, the American people, shall withhold the requisite means, or, in some authoritative manner, direct the contrary. I trust this will not be regarded as a menace, but only as the declared purpose of the Union that it will constitutionally defend, and maintain itself.

In doing this there needs to be no bloodshed or violence; and there shall be none, unless it be forced upon the national authority. The power the confided to me, will be used to hold, occupy, and possess the property, and places belonging to the government, and to collect the duties and imposts; but beyond what may be necessary for these objects, there will be no invasion—no using of force against, or among the people anywhere. Where hostility to the United States, in any interior locality, shall be so great and so universal, as to prevent competent resident citizens from holding the Federal offices, there will be no attempt to force obnoxious strangers among the people for that object. While the strict legal right may exist in the government to enforce the exercise of these offices, the attempt to do so would be so irritating, and so nearly impracticable with all, that I deem it better to forego, for the time, the uses of such offices.

The mails, unless repelled, will continue to be furnished in all parts of the Union. So far as possible, the people everywhere shall have that sense of perfect security which is most favorable to calm thought and reflection. The course here indicated will be followed, unless current events, and experience, shall show a modification, or change, to be proper; and in every case and exigency, my best discretion will be exercised, according to circumstances actually existing, and with a view and a hope of a peaceful solution of the national troubles, and the restoration of fraternal sympathies and affections.

That there are persons in one section, or another who seek to destroy the Union at all events, and are glad of any pretext to do it, I will neither affirm or deny; but if there be such, I need address no word to them. To those, however, who really love the Union, may I not speak?

Before entering upon so grave a matter as the destruction of our national fabric, with all its benefits, its memories, and its hopes, would it not be wise to ascertain precisely why we do it? Will you hazard so desperate a step, while there is any possibility that any portion of the ills you fly from, have no real existence? Will you, while the certain ills you fly to, are greater than all the real ones you fly from? Will you risk the commission of so fearful a mistake?

All profess to be content in the Union, if all constitutional rights can be maintained. Is it true, then, that any right, plainly written in the Constitution, has been denied? I think not. Happily the human mind is so constituted, that no party can reach to the audacity of doing this. Think, if you can, of a single instance in which a plainly written provision of the Constitution has ever been denied. If, by the mere force of numbers, a majority should deprive a minority of any clearly written constitutional right, it might, in a moral point of view, justify revolution—certainly would, if such right were a vital one. But such is not our case. All the vital rights of minorities, and of individuals, are so plainly assured to them, by affirmations and negations, guarranties and prohibitions, in the Constitution, that controversies never arise concerning them. But no organic law can ever be framed with a provision specifically applicable to every question which may occur in practical administration. No foresight can anticipate, nor any document of reasonable length contain express provisions for all possible questions. Shall fugitives from labor be surrendered by national or by State authority? The Constitution does not expressly say. May Congress prohibit slavery in the territories? The Constitution does not expressly say. Must Congress protect slavery in the territories? The Constitution does not expressly say.

From questions of this class spring all our constitutional controversies, and we divide upon them into majorities and minorities. If the minority will not acquiesce, the majority must, or the government must cease. There is no other alternative; for continuing the government, is acquiescence on one side or the other. If a minority, in such case, will secede rather than acquiesce, they make a precedent which, in turn, will divide and ruin them; for a minority of their own will secede from them, whenever a majority refuses to be controlled by such minority. For instance, why may not any portion of a new confederacy, a year or two hence, arbitrarily secede again, precisely as portions of the present Union now claim to secede from it. All who cherish disunion sentiments, are now being educated to the exact temper of doing this. Is there such perfect identity of interests among the States to compose a new Union, as to produce harmony only, and prevent renewed secession?

Plainly, the central idea of secession, is the essence of anarchy. A majority, held in restraint by constitutional checks, and limitations, and always changing easily, with deliberate changes of popular opinions and sentiments, is the only true sovereign of a free people. Whoever rejects it, does, of necessity, fly to anarchy or to despotism. Unanimity is impossible; the rule of a minority, as a permanent arrangement, is wholly inadmissable; so that, rejecting the majority principle, anarchy, or despotism in some form, is all that is left. . . .

One section of our country believes slavery is right, and ought to be extended, while the other believes it is wrong, and ought not to be extended. This is the only substantial dispute. The fugitive slave clause of the Constitution, and the law for the suppression of the foreign slave trade, are each as well enforced, perhaps, as any law can ever be in a community where the moral sense of the people imperfectly supports the law itself. The great body of the people abide by the dry legal obligation in both cases, and a few break over in each. This, I think, cannot be perfectly cured; and it would be worse in both cases after the separation of the sections, than before. The foreign slave trade, now imperfectly suppressed, would be ultimately revived without restriction, in one section; while fugitive slaves, now only partially surrendered, would not be surrendered at all, by the other.

Physically speaking, we cannot separate. We cannot remove our respective sections from each other, nor build an impassable wall between them. A husband and wife may be divorced, and go out of the presence, and beyond the reach of each other; but the different parts of our country cannot do this. They cannot but remain face to face; and intercourse, either amicable or hostile, must continue between them. Is it possible then to make that intercourse more advantageous, or more satisfactory, after separation than before? Can aliens make treaties easier than friends can make laws? Can treaties be more faithfully enforced between aliens, than laws can among friends? Suppose you go to war, you cannot fight always; and when, after much loss on both sides, and no gain on either, you cease fighting, the identical old questions, as to terms of intercourse, are again upon you.

This country, with its institutions, belongs to the people who inhabit it. Whenever they shall grow weary of the existing government, they can exercise their constitutional right of amending it, or their revolutionary right to dismember, or overthrow it. I can not be ignorant of the fact that many worthy, and patriotic citizens are desirous of having the national constitution amended. While I make no recommendation of amendments, I fully recognize the rightful authority of the people over the whole subject, to be exercised in either of the modes prescribed in the instrument itself; and I should, under existing circumstances, favor, rather than oppose, a fair opportunity being afforded the people to act upon it.

I will venture to add that, to me, the convention mode seems preferable, in that it allows amendments to originate with the people themselves, instead of only permitting them to take, or reject, propositions, originated by others, not especially chosen for the purpose, and which might not be precisely such, as they would wish to either accept or refuse. I understand a proposed amendment to the Constitution—which amendment, however, I have not seen, has passed Congress, to the effect that the federal government, shall never interfere with the domestic institutions of the States, including that of persons held to service. To avoid misconstruction of what I have said, I depart from my purpose not to speak of particular amendments, so far as to say that, holding such a provision to now be implied constitutional law, I have no objection to its being made express, and irrevocable.

The Chief Magistrate derives all his authority from the people, and they have conferred none upon him to fix terms for the separation of the States. The people themselves can do this also if they choose; but the executive, as such, has nothing to do with it. His duty is to administer the present government, as it came to his hands, and to transmit it, unimpaired by him, to his successor.

Why should there not be a patient confidence in the ultimate justice of the people? Is there any better, or equal hope, in the world? In our present differences, is either party without faith of being in the right? If the Almighty Ruler of nations, with his eternal truth and justice, be on your side of the North, or on yours of the South, that truth, and that justice, will surely prevail, by the judgment of this great tribunal, the American people.

By the frame of the government under which we live, this same people have wisely given their public servants but little power for mischief; and have, with equal wisdom, provided for the return of that little to their own hands at very short intervals.

While the people retain their virtue, and vigilence, no administration, by any extreme of wickedness or folly, can very seriously injure the government, in the short space of four years.

My countrymen, one and all, think calmly and well, upon this whole subject. Nothing valuable can be lost by taking time. If there be an object to hurry any of you, in hot haste, to a step which you would never take deliberately, that object will be frustrated by taking time; but no good object can be frustrated by it. Such of you as are now dissatisfied, still have the old Constitution unimpaired, and, on the sensitive point, the laws of your own framing under it; while the new administration will have no immediate power, if it would, to change either. If it were admitted that you who are dissatisfied, hold the right side in the dispute, there still is no single good reason for precipitate action. Intelligence, patriotism, Christianity, and a firm reliance on Him, who has never yet forsaken this favored land, are still competent to adjust, in the best way, all our present difficulty.

In your hands, my dissatisfied fellow countrymen, and not in mine, is the momentous issue of civil war. The government will not assail you. You can have no conflict, without being yourselves the aggressors. You have no oath registered in Heaven to destroy the government, while I shall have the most solemn one to "preserve, protect and defend" it.

I am loth to close. We are not enemies, but friends. We must not be enemies. Though passion may have strained, it must not break our bonds of affection. The mystic chords of memory, stretching from every battle-field, and patriot grave, to every living heart and hearthstone, all over this broad land, will yet swell the chorus of the Union, when again touched, as surely they will be, by the better angels of our nature.

DRAWING CONCLUSIONS:

1. What does this document reveal about Lincoln's position on the slavery issue upon taking office?
2. What does this document reveal about Lincoln's political priorities upon taking office? On what issues was he willing to compromise? On what issues did he take a hard line?

2.6 JOINT CONGRESSIONAL RESOLUTION ON WAR AIMS (JULY 25, 1861)

On April 12, 1861, hostilities commenced when Confederate forces in Charleston, South Carolina, opened fire on a federal military installation at Fort Sumter in the city's harbor. In response, Lincoln called upon the states to provide troops to suppress the rebellion. (The United States had a very small standing army at the time.) Forced to choose sides, four slave states rejected Lincoln's call for troops and quickly voted to join the Confederacy, making for a total of eleven Confederate states. By the summer of 1861, it was clear that the rebellion had escalated into full-scale civil war. In July 1861, the US Congress (overwhelming dominated by the Republican Party after the resignation of members from the seceded states) approved a resolution establishing the aims of the Union war effort. This resolution provides evidence of how federal policymakers (including anti-slavery Republicans) understood the goals of the war in its early days.

GUIDING QUESTIONS:

1. What, according this congressional resolution, were Union forces fighting for?
2. What position did the Congress take on the slavery issue in its resolution on war aims?

JOINT CONGRESSIONAL WAR AIMS RESOLUTION

JULY 25, 1861

Resolved, That the present deplorable civil war has been forced upon the country by the disunionists of the southern States now in revolt against the constitutional Government and in arms around the capital; that in this national emergency Congress, banishing all feeling of mere passion or resentment, will recollect only its duty to the whole country; that this war is not prosecuted upon our part in any spirit of oppression, nor for any purpose of conquest or subjugation, nor purpose of overthrowing or interfering with rights or established institutions of those States, but to defend and maintain the supremacy of the Constitution and all laws made in pursuance thereof, and to preserve the Union, with all the dignity, equality, and rights of the several States unimpaired; that as soon as these objects are accomplished the war ought to cease.

DRAWING CONCLUSIONS:

1. What does the resolution on war aims reveal about the stance of the Republican-dominated Congress on the slavery issue early in the war?

From *Journal of the Senate,* 37th Congress, 1st Session, July 25, 1861.

THE "CONTRABAND" ISSUE

Regardless of the stance taken by the Lincoln administration and the Congress, the large numbers of slaves that escaped to Union lines in the early months of the war forced federal officials to address the issue of slavery. The Confederate military employed large numbers of slaves in such tasks as building fortifications and helping to move supplies. Federal officials determined that runaway slaves who had been forced to labor on behalf of the Confederate war effort would be treated as "contraband"—enemy property seized under generally accepted rules of war. This, of course, left the status of other runaway slaves undetermined.

3.1 CORRESPONDENCE BETWEEN BENJAMIN BUTLER, WINFIELD SCOTT, AND SIMON CAMERON (MAY 1861)

Six weeks after the attack on Fort Sumter, three enslaved men compelled to construct Confederate fortifications in coastal Virginia escaped to Union lines at Fortress Monroe, under the command of General Benjamin F. Butler. (Prior to the war, Butler had been a pro-slavery Democratic politician in Massachusetts.) Under the federal fugitive slave act, Butler was required to return the men to their legal owner. Butler, however, chose not to do so. Over the next few days, many more slaves arrived at Fort Monroe, including women and children. In the following exchange of letters, Butler informs General Winfield Scott (the commander of all Union forces) of developments at Fort Monroe and asks for guidance. In the final letter, Secretary of War Simon Cameron provides Butler with the guidance he has asked for.

GUIDING QUESTIONS:

1. What dilemmas did the arrival of runaway slaves pose for Benjamin Butler? How did Butler respond to these dilemmas? Why did Butler respond in these ways?
2. What questions did Butler have for his commanding officer?
3. What answers did Secretary of War Cameron give to Butler's questions?
4. Why did Secretary of War Cameron give these answers?

BENJAMIN F. BUTLER TO WINFIELD SCOTT

HEADQUARTERS DEPARTMENT OF VIRGINIA, FORT MONROE, MAY 24, 1861.

Lieutenant General WINFIELD SCOTT:

. . .

Saturday, May 25.—I had written thus far when I was called away to meet Major Cary, of the active Virginia volunteers, upon questions which have arisen of very considerable importance both in a military and political aspect and which I beg leave to submit herewith.

On Thursday night three negroes, field hands belonging to Colonel Charles K. Mallory now in command of the secession forces in this district, delivered themselves up to my picket guard and as I learned from the report of the officer of the guard in the morning had been detained by him. I immediately gave personal attention to the matter and found satisfactory evidence that these men were about to be taken to Carolina for the purpose of aiding the secession forces there; that two of them left wives and children (one a free woman) here; that the other had left his master from fear that he would be called upon to take part in the rebel armies. Satisfied of these facts from cautious examination of each of the negroes apart from the others I determined for the present and until better advised as these men were very serviceable and I had great need of labor in my quartermaster's department to avail myself of their services, and that I would send a receipt to Colonel Mallory that I had so taken them as I would for any other property of a private citizen which the exigencies of the service seemed to require to be taken by me, and

From *The War of the Rebellion: A Compilation of the Official Records of the Union and Confederate Armies*, Series 2, Volume 1, 752.

especially property that was designed, adapted and about to be used against the United States.

As this is but an individual instance in a course of policy which may be required to be pursued with regard to this species of property I have detailed to the lieutenant-general this case and ask his direction. I am credibly informed that the negroes in this neighborhood are now being employed in the erection of batteries and other works by the rebels which it would be nearly or quite impossible to construct without their labor. Shall they be allowed the use of this property against the United States and we not be allowed its use in aid of the United States?

. . .

Major Cary demanded to know with regard to the negroes what course I intended to pursue. I answered him substantially as I have written above when he desired to know if I did not feel myself bound by my constitutional obligations to deliver up fugitives under the fugitive-slave act. To this I replied that the fugitive-slave act did not affect a foreign country which Virginia claimed to be and that she must reckon it one of the infelicities of her position that in so far at least she was taken at her word; that in Maryland, a loyal State, fugitives from service had been returned, and that even now although so much pressed by my necessities for the use of these men of Colonel Mallory's yet if their master would come to the fort and take the oath of allegiance to the Constitution of the United States I would deliver the men up to him and endeavor to hire their services of him if he desired to part with them. To this Major Cary responded that Colonel Mallory was absent.

. . .

Trusting that these dispositions and movements will meet the approval of the lieutenant-general and begging pardon for the detailed length of this dispatch, I have the honor to be, most respectfully, your obedient servant,

BENJ. F. BUTLER,
Major-General, Commanding.

BENJAMIN F. BUTLER TO WINFIELD SCOTT

HEADQUARTERS DEPARTMENT OF VIRGINIA, FORT MONROE, MAY 27, 1861.

Lieutenant-General SCOTT.

SIR: . . . Since I wrote my last dispatch the question in regard to slave property is becoming one of very serious magnitude. The inhabitants of Virginia are using their negroes in the batteries and are preparing to send the women and children south. The escapes from them are very numerous and a squad has come in this morning to my pickets bringing their women and children. Of course these cannot be dealt with upon the theory on which I designed to treat the services of able-bodied men and women who might come within my lines, and of which I gave you a detailed account in my last dispatch. I am in the utmost doubt what to do with this species of property. Up to this time I have had come within my lines men and women with their children, entire families, each family belonging to the same owner. I have therefore determined to employ as I can do very profitably the able-bodied persons in the party, issuing proper food for the support of all and charging against their services the expense of care and sustenance of the non-laborers, keeping a strict and accurate account as well of the services as of the expenditure, having the worth of the services and the cost of the expenditure determined by a board of survey to be hereafter detailed. I know of no other manner in which to dispose of this subject and the questions connected therewith. As a matter of property to the insurgents it will be of very great moment, the number that I now have amounting as I am informed to what in good times would be of the value of $60,000. Twelve of these negroes I am informed have escaped from the batteries on Sewall's Point which this morning fired upon my expedition as it passed by out of range. As a means of offense therefore in the enemy's hands these negroes when able-bodied are of the last importance. Without them the batteries could not have been erected, at least for many weeks. As a military question it would seem to be a measure of necessity to deprive their masters of their services. How can this be done? As a political question and question of humanity can I receive the services of a father and mother and not take the children? Of the humanitarian aspect I have no doubt; of the political one I have no right to judge. . . .

Very respectfully, your obedient servant,
B. F. BUTLER.

SIMON CAMERON TO BENJAMIN F. BUTLER

WASHINGTON, MAY 30, 1861.

Major-General BUTLER:

SIR: Your action in respect to the negroes who came in your lines from the service of the rebels is approved.

The Department is sensible of the embarrassment which must surround officers conducting military operations in a State by the laws of which slavery is sanctioned. The Government cannot recognize the rejection by any State of its federal obligations nor can it refuse the performance of the federal obligations resting upon itself. Among these federal obligations, however, none can be more important than that of suppressing and dispersing armed combinations formed for the purpose of overthrowing its whole constitutional authority. While therefore you will permit no interference by the persons under your command with the relations of persons held to service under the laws of any State you will on the other hand so long as any State within which your military operations are conducted is under the control of such armed combinations refrain from surrendering to alleged masters any persons who may come within your lines. You will employ such persons in the service to which they may be best adapted, keeping an account of the labor by them performed, of the value of it and of the expense of their maintenance. The question of their final disposition will be reserved for future determination.

SIMON CAMERON,
Secretary of War.

DRAWING CONCLUSIONS:

1. What does this exchange of letters reveal about the impact of escaped slaves on Union military officers such as Benjamin Butler and federal policymakers such as Simon Cameron?

From *The War of the Rebellion: A Compilation of the Official Records of the Union and Confederate Armies*, Series 2, Volume 1, 754–755.

3.2 CORRESPONDENCE BETWEEN BENJAMIN BUTLER AND SIMON CAMERON (JULY–AUGUST, 1861)

In July of 1861, General Butler was forced to evacuate the town of Hampton, Virginia, which he had earlier occupied. While under Union control, Hampton had become a magnet for runaway slaves from neighboring areas of coastal Virginia. As Butler's forces left Hampton, the hundreds of black men, women, and children who had taken refuge there were forced to abandon their makeshift homes to remain behind Union lines. In this exchange, Butler asks Secretary of War Cameron for guidance on the policies he should adopt toward the growing number of refugees under his authority. This second set of letters between Butler and Cameron is particularly interesting as an illustration of the evolution of the formerly pro-slavery Butler's thoughts and feelings toward the South's "peculiar institution."

GUIDING QUESTIONS:

1. What dilemmas did the growing number of escaped slaves under his authority pose for Butler?
2. How did Butler's interactions with escaped slaves affect his feelings on issues of slavery and race?
3. What guidance did Secretary of War Cameron give Butler with regard to runaway slaves under Butler's authority? Why did Cameron give this advice?
4. What issues, if any, did Cameron's message to Butler leave unresolved?

BENJAMIN F. BUTLER TO SIMON CAMERON

HEADQUARTERS DEPARTMENT OF VIRGINIA, FORTRESS MONROE, JULY 30, 1861

Hon. Simon Cameron, Secretary of War:

SIR: By an order received on the morning of the 26th of July, from Major-Gen. Dix, by a telegraphic order from Lieutenant-General Scott, I was commanded to forward, of the troops of this Department, four regiments and a half, including Colonel Baker's California Regiment, to Washington, via Baltimore. This order reached me at 2 o'clock A.M., by special boat from Baltimore. Believing that it emanated because of some pressing exigency for the defense of Washington, I issued my orders before daybreak for the embarkation of the troops, sending those who were among the very best regiments I had. In the course of the following day they were all embarked for Baltimore, with the exception of some four hundred, for whom I had not transportation, although I had all the transport force in the hands of the Quartermaster here, to aid the Bay line of steamers, which, by the same order from the lieutenant-general, was directed to furnish transportation. Up to and at the time of the order I had been preparing for an advance movement, by which I hoped to cripple the resources of the enemy at Yorktown, and especially by seizing a large quantity of negroes, who were being pressed into their service in building the intrenchments there. I had five days previously been enabled to mount, for

From *Private and Official Correspondence of Gen. Benjamin F. Butler: During the Civil War Period*, vol. 1 (Norwood, MA: Plimpton Press, 1917), 185–188.

the first time, the first company of Light Artillery, which I had been empowered to raise, and they had but a single rifled cannon, an iron six-pounder. Of course, everything must, and did yield to the supposed exigency and the orders. This ordering away the troops from this department, while it weakened the posts at Newport's News, necessitated the withdrawal of the troops from Hampton, where I was then throwing up intrenched works, to enable me to hold the town with a small force, while I advanced up the York or James River. In the village of Hampton there were a large number of negroes, composed, in a great measure, of women and children of the men who had fled thither within my lines for protection, who had escaped from marauding parties of rebels who had been gathering up able-bodied blacks to aid them in constructing their batteries on the James and York Rivers. I had employed the men in Hampton in tin owing up intrenchments, and they were working zealously and efficiently at that duty, saving our soldiers from that labor, under the gleam of the mid-day sun. The women were earning substantially their own subsistence in washing, marketing, and taking care of the clothes of the soldiers, and rations were being served out to the men who worked for the support of the children. But by the evacuation of Hampton, rendered necessary by the withdrawal of troops, leaving me scarcely five thousand men outside the Fort, including the force at Newport News, all these black people were obliged to break up their homes at Hampton, fleeing across the creek within my lines for protection and support. Indeed it was a most distressing sight to see these poor creatures, who had trusted to the protection of the arms of the United States, and who aided the troops of the United States in their enterprise, to be thus obliged to flee from their homes, and the homes of their masters, who had deserted them, and become not fugitives from fear of the return of the rebel soldiery, who had threatened to shoot the men who had wrought for us, and to carry off the women who had served us to a worse than Egyptian bondage. I have therefore now within the Peninsula, this side of Hampton Creek, nine hundred negroes, three hundred of whom are able-bodied men, thirty of whom are men substantially past hard labor, one hundred and seventy-five

women, two hundred and twenty-five children under the age of ten years, and one hundred and seventy between ten and eighteen years, and many more coming in. The questions which this state of facts present are very embarrassing.

First—What shall be done with them? and, *Second,* What is their state and condition? Upon these questions I desire the instructions of the Department.

The first question, however, may perhaps be answered by considering the last. Are these men, women, and children, slaves? Are they free? Is their condition that of men, women, and children, or that of property, or is it a mixed relation? What their status was under the Constitution and laws, we all know. What has been the effect of rebellion and a state of war upon that status? When I adopted the theory of treating the able-bodied negro fit to work in the trenches, as property liable to be used in aid of rebellion, and so contraband of war, that condition of things was in so far met as I then and still believe, on a legal and constitutional basis. But now a new series of questions arise. Passing by women, the children certainly cannot be treated on that basis; if property, they must be considered the incumbrance, rather than the auxiliary of an army, and of course, in no possible legal relation, could be treated as contraband. Are they property? If they were so they have been left by their masters and owners, deserted, thrown away, abandoned, like the wrecked vessel upon the ocean. Their former possessors and owners have causelessly, traitorously, rebelliously, and, to carry out the figure practically abandoned them to be swallowed up by the winter storm of starvation. If property, do they not become the property of the salvors? But we, their salvors, do not need and will not hold such property, and will assume no such ownership. Has not, therefore, all proprietary relation ceased? Have they not become thereupon men, women and children? No longer under ownership of any kind, the fearful relics of fugitive masters, have they not by their masters' acts and the state of war assumed the condition, which we hold to be the normal one, of those made in God's image? Is not every constitutional, legal and moral requirement, as well to the runaway master as their relinquished slaves, thus answered? I confess that my own mind is compelled by this reasoning to look upon them as men and women. If not free born, yet free, manumitted, sent forth from the hand that held them never to be reclaimed.

Of course, if this reasoning thus imperfectly set forth is correct, my duty as a humane man is very plain. I should take the same care of these men, women and children, houseless, homeless and unprovided for, as I would of the same number of men, women and children who, for their attachment to the Union, had been driven or allowed to flee from the Confederate States. I should have no doubt on this question, had I not seen it stated that an order had been issued by Gen. McDowell, in his department, substantially forbidding all fugitive slaves from coming within his lines or being harbored there. Is that order to be enforced in all military departments? If so, who are to be considered fugitive slaves? Is a slave to be considered fugitive whose master runs away and leaves him? Is it forbidden to the troops to aid or harbor within their lines the negro children who are found therein, or is the soldier, when his march has destroyed their means of subsistence, to allow them to starve because he has driven off the rebel master? Now, shall the commander of regiment or battalion sit in judgment upon the question, whether any given black man has fled from his master, or his master fled from him? Indeed, how are the free born to be distinguished? Is one any more or less a fugitive slave because he has labored on the rebel intrenchments? If he has so labored, if I understand it, he is to be harbored. By the reception of which are the rebels most to be distressed, by taking those who have wrought all their rebel masters desired, masked their battery, or those who have refused to labor, and left the battery unmasked?

I have very decided opinions upon the subject of this order. It does not become me to criticise it, and I write in no spirit of criticism, but simply to explain the full difficulties that surround the enforcing it. If the enforcement of that order becomes the policy of the Government, I, as a soldier, shall be bound to enforce it steadfastly, if not cheerfully.

But if left to my own discretion, as you may have gathered from my reasoning, I should take a widely different course from that which it indicates.

In a loyal State I would put down a servile insurrection. In a state of rebellion I would confiscate that which was used to oppose my arms, and take all that property, which constituted the wealth of that State, and furnished the means by which the war is prosecuted, besides being the cause of the war; and if, in so doing, it should be objected that human beings were brought to the free enjoyment of life, liberty and the pursuit of happiness, such objections might not require much consideration.

Pardon me for addressing the secretary of war directly upon this question, as it involves some political considerations, as well as propriety of military action.

Benj. F. Butler

SIMON CAMERON TO BENJAMIN F. BUTLER

WASHINGTON, AUGUST 8, 1861.

Major General B. F. BUTLER,
        Commanding Department of Virginia, Fortress Monroe:

GENERAL: The important question of the proper disposition to be made of fugitives from service in States in insurrection against the Federal Government to which you have again directed my attention in your letter of July 30 has received my most attentive consideration.

It is the desire of the President that all existing rights in all the States be fully respected and maintained. The war now prosecuted on the part of the Federal Government is a war for the Union and for the preservation of all constitutional rights of States and the citizens of the States in the Union. Hence no question can arise as to fugitives from service within the States and Territories in which the authority of the Union is fully acknowledge[d]. The ordinary forms of judicial proceeding which must be respected

From *The War of the Rebellion: A Compilation of the Official Records of the Union and Confederate Armies*, Series 2, Volume 1, 761–762.

by military and civil authorities alike will suffice for the enforcement of all legal claims. But in States wholly or partially under insurrectionary control where the laws of the United States are so far opposed and resisted that they cannot be effectually enforced it is obvious that rights dependent on the execution of those laws must temporarily fail; and it is equally obvious operations are conducted must be necessarily subordinated to the military exigencies created by the insurrection if not wholly forfeited by the treasonable conduct of parties claiming them. To this general rule rights to services can form no exception.

The act of Congress approved August 6, 1861, declares that if persons held to service shall be employed in hostility to the United States the right to their services shall be forfeited and such persons shall be discharged therefrom. It follows of necessity that no claim can be recognized by the military authorities of the Union to the services of such persons when fugitives.

A more difficult question is presented in respect to persons escaping from the service of loyal masters. It is quite apparent that the laws of the State under which only the services of such fugitives can be claimed must needs be wholly or almost wholly suspended as to remedies by the insurrection and the military measures necessitated by it. And it is equally apparent that the substitution of military for judicial measures for the enforcement of such claims must be attended by great inconveniences, embarrassments and injuries.

Under these circumstances it seems quite clear that the substantial rights of loyal masters will be best protected by receiving such fugitives as well as fugitives from disloyal masters into the service of the United States, and employing them under such organizations and in such occupations as circumstances may suggest or require. Of course a record should be kept showing the name and description of the fugitives, the name and the character as loyal or disloyal of the master, and such facts as may be necessary to a correct understanding of the circumstances of each case after tranquility shall have been restored. Upon the return of peace Congress will doubtless properly provide for all the persons thus received into the service of the Union and for just compensation to loyal masters. In this way only it would seem can the duty and safety of the Government and the just rights of all be fully reconciled and harmonized.

You will therefore consider yourself as instructed to govern your future action in respect to fugitives from service by the principles herein stated, and will report from time to time—and at least twice in each month—your action in the premises to this Department. You will, however, neither authorize nor permit any interference by the troops under your command with the servants of peaceful citizens in house or field, nor will you in any way encourage such servants to leave the lawful service of their masters, nor will you except in cases where the public safety may seem to require prevent the voluntary return of any fugitive to the service from which he may have escaped.

I am, general, very respectfully, your obedient servant,

SIMON CAMERON,
Secretary of War.

DRAWING CONCLUSIONS:

1. What does this exchange of letters reveal about the impact of escaped slaves on Union military officers such as Benjamin Butler and federal policymakers such as Simon Cameron?

3.3 FIRST CONFISCATION ACT
(AUGUST 6, 1861)

In the War Aims Resolution of July 1861, the United States Congress declared that it had no intention of interfering with the institution of slavery. A month later, however, the very same Congress passed the First Confiscation Act, which declared that under certain circumstances slave owners would forfeit their property right in their slaves.

GUIDING QUESTIONS:

1. Under what circumstances does the First Confiscation Act declare the property rights of slave owners to be forfeited?
2. Why would a Congress that had just declared it had no intention of interfering with the institution of slavery enact a law that freed certain slaves?

AN ACT TO CONFISCATE PROPERTY USED FOR INSURRECTIONARY PURPOSES

Be it enacted by the Senate and House of Representatives of the United States of America in Congress assembled, That if, during the present or any future insurrection against the Government of the United States, after the President of the United States shall have declared, by proclamation, that the laws of the United States are opposed, and the execution thereof obstructed, by combinations too powerful to be suppressed by the ordinary course of judicial proceedings, or by the power vested in the marshals by law, any person or persons, his, her, or their agent, attorney, or employeé, shall purchase or acquire, sell or give, any property of whatsoever kind or description, with intent to use or employ the same, or suffer the same to be used or employed, in aiding, abetting, or promoting such insurrection or resistance to the laws, or any person or persons engaged therein; or if any person or persons, being the owner or owners of any such property, shall knowingly use or employ, or consent to the use or employment of the same as aforesaid, all such property is hereby declared to be lawful subject of prize and capture wherever found; and it shall be the duty of the President of the United States to cause the same to be seized, confiscated, and condemned.

SEC. 2. *And be it further enacted,* That such prizes and capture shall be condemned in the district or circuit court of the United States having jurisdiction of the amount, or in admiralty in any district in which the same may be seized, or into which they may be taken and proceedings first instituted.

SEC. 3. *And be it further enacted,* That the Attorney-General, or any district attorney of the United States in which said property may at the time be, may institute the proceedings of condemnation, and in such case they shall be wholly for the benefit of the United States; or any person may file an information with such attorney, in which case the proceedings shall be for the use of such informer and the United States in equal parts.

SEC. 4. *And be it further enacted,* That whenever hereafter, during the present insurrection against the Government of the United States, any person claimed to be held to labor or service under the law of any State, shall be required or permitted by the person to whom such labor or service is claimed to be due, or by the lawful agent of such person, to take up arms against the United States, or shall be

From *The Statutes at Large, Treaties, and Proclamations of the United States of America,* 37th Congress, 1st Session, 319.

required or permitted by the person to whom such labor or service is claimed to be due, or his lawful agent, to work or to be employed in or upon any fort, navy yard, dock, armory, ship, entrenchment, or in any military or naval service whatsoever, against the Government and lawful authority of the United States, then, and in every such case, the person to whom such labor or service is claimed to be due shall forfeit his claim to such labor, any law of the State or of the United States to the contrary notwithstanding. And whenever thereafter the person claiming such labor or service shall seek to enforce his claim, it shall be a full and sufficient answer to such claim that the person whose service or labor is claimed had been employed in hostile service against the Government of the United States, contrary to the provisions of this act.

APPROVED, **August 6, 1861.**

DRAWING CONCLUSIONS:

1. What does the First Confiscation Act reveal about the impact of the war on policymaker's thinking about slavery?

3.4 MAJOR GEORGE E. WARING TO GENERAL HENRY W. HALLECK (DECEMBER 19, 1861)

Not all federal commanders proved as sympathetic to escaped slaves as did Benjamin Butler. General Henry W. Halleck, commanding Union troops in the western theater, in fact, issued an order in November 1861 barring fugitives from entering the lines of any camp under his command. Enforcing this order, though, proved difficult. In this letter, one of Halleck's subordinates, Major George E. Waring, writes the general and describes the difficulties Halleck's order posed for him. The letter also provides a window into the ways that fugitive slaves within Union lines advocated for their own interests.

GUIDING QUESTIONS:

1. What reasons does Major Waring give in this letter for his reluctance to enforce General Halleck's order barring fugitive slaves from Union camps under his command?
2. What strategies did escaped slaves employ to remain in Major Waring's camp? Why were these strategies effective?

CAMP HALLECK NEAR ROLLA MO. DEC 19TH 61

General: In obedience to the order contained in your circular (No. 2), received this day, I beg to report that on the receipt of your order No. 23 communicating Gen. Order No. 3, from the Commanding General, ordering fugitive slaves to be excluded from the lines, I caused all negroes in my camp to be examined, and it was reported to me that they all stoutly asserted that they were free.

Since that time a woman employed in my own mess as a cook has been claimed by one Captain Holland as the fugitive slave of his father-in-law. In compliance with your order, to that end, which he produced, she was given up to him. Since the receipt of your circular today, I have again caused an investigation to be thoroughly made which has resulted as in the first instance.

I beg now, General, to ask for your instructions in the matter. These negroes all claim and insist they are *free*. Some of them, I have no question, are so; others

I have as little doubt have been slaves,—but no one is here to prove it, and I hesitate to take so serious a responsibility as to decide, arbitrarily, in the absence of any direct evidence, that they are such.

If I turn them away, I inflict great hardship upon them, as they would be homeless and helpless. Furthermore, such a course would occasion much personal inconvenience and sincere regret, to other officers no less than to myself. These people are mainly our servants, and we can get no others. They have been employed in this capacity for some time—long enough for us to like them as servants, to find them useful and trustworthy, and to feel an interest in their welfare.

The Commanding General, in his letter to Col. Blair, (as published in the Missouri Democrat of the 16th inst), says—in explanation of General order No 3.—"Unauthorized persons, black or white, free or slave, must be kept out of our camps." The negroes in my camp are employed, in accordance with the Army

From Ira Berlin et al., eds., *Free At Last: A Documentary History of Slavery, Freedom, and the Civil War* (New York: The New Press, 1992), 27–29.

Regulations, as officers servants, teamsters, and hospital attendants, and, with the exception of one little child are such as we are authorized to have in the camp. It seems to me that they are without the pale of the order and the *intention* of the Commanding General, and I trust that I may be excused for awaiting more explicit instructions before doing what may be an extra-official act—at which my private feelings revolt.

I recognize the fact that obedience to Gen. Orders No. 3 is a part of my military duty, and I shall unflinchingly comply with it in the consciousness that I am in no way responsible therefore; but I *am* personally responsible for my decision, when it is to affect the happiness and security of others.

May I ask you, General, to relieve me of this responsibility by giving me your final decision at your earliest convenience. Very Respectfully Your Obedient Servant

Geo. E. Waring, Jr.

DRAWING CONCLUSIONS:

1. What does this letter reveal about the ways individual slaves pursued their own freedom prior to the issuing of the Emancipation Proclamation?
2. What does this letter reveal about choices federal officers faced when confronted by the arrival of large numbers of fugitive slaves at their lines?

3.5   TESTIMONY OF SAMUEL ELLIOT (1873)

Samuel Elliot had been held in bondage in the state of Georgia. In 1861, his master entered the Confederate Army and took Elliot with him to Virginia, where he was stationed. Elliot was present for some battles in the vicinity of Fort Monroe during the early phases of the spring 1862 Peninsula Campaign. After eleven months, Elliot and his master returned home to Georgia. In the following testimony, provided to a federal investigation commission following the war, Elliot describes how other slaves (including his own son) reacted to the news he brought back home with him from Virginia.

GUIDING QUESTIONS:

1. What information does it appear that Elliot shared with fellow slaves in his home community?
2. How did those in his home community respond to this news?

TESTIMONY OF SAMUEL ELLIOT BEFORE THE SOUTHERN CLAIMS COMMISSION

[MCINTOSH, GA. JULY 17, 1873]

My name is Samuel Elliott I was born in Liberty County a Slave and became free when the Army came into the County. I belonged to Maybank Jones. I am 54 years old. I reside at Lauralview in Liberty County. I am a farmer. I am the Claimant in this Case. . . .

. . . I resided from the 1st of April 1861 to the 1st of June 1865 where I live now at Lauralview. I worked for my master all the time. I changed my business at one time when I was with my master as a waiter—in the rebel service I was with him Eleven month. I came home with him. I told my son what was going on—he with 11 more ran off and joined the Army (the Yankee Army) on St Catherine Island. I dont remember the Year but it was soon after the battle at Williamsburgh Va, and before the 7 days battle near Chickahomony. I mean that was the time I came home with my master. I was with him at Yorktown—Soon after I came home My son with 11 others ran away & joined the Union Army. My Master had me taken up tied me and tried to make me tell "What made them ran off" I had to lie about it to keep from getting killed. the 11 slaves belonged to My Master Jones that stoped the slave owners from sending or taking slave into the Army as waiters or anything else. it stoped it in our neighborhood.

DRAWING CONCLUSIONS:

1. What does Elliot's testimony reveal about the factors that led many southern slaves to leave their homes to seek Union lines in the period before the Emancipation Proclamation?

From Ira Berlin et al., ed., *Freedom: A Documentary History of Emancipation, 1861–1867*, Series I, Vol. 1, *The Destruction of Slavery* (Cambridge: Cambridge University Press, 1985), 146.

3.6   SUSIE KING TAYLOR, EXCERPT FROM *REMINISCENCES OF MY LIFE IN CAMP* (1902)

Susie King Taylor was born a slave in coastal Georgia in 1848. As a young girl, she was allowed by her master to move to the town of Savannah to live with her grandmother, who appears to have been freed earlier by her master. Her grandmother enrolled Taylor in an illegal school, where she learned to read and write. (Teaching a slave to read or write was a violation of Georgia law.) In 1862, federal forces occupied portions of the Georgia coastline, and Taylor (along with many other slaves) escaped to Union lines. During the war, Taylor served as a nurse and laundress to a black Union regiment and also ran literacy classes for African American children. (Some adults also attended.) Toward the end of her life, Taylor published a memoir of her experiences in war entitled *Reminiscences of My Life in Camp*. In the excerpt provided here, Taylor provides an account of the outbreak of the war and her escape to Union lines.

GUIDING QUESTIONS:

1. How did Susie King Taylor and members of her family react to the outbreak of the Civil War?
2. Why did Susie King Taylor and members of her family abandon their homes to seek the Union lines on St. Catherine's Island?

EXCERPT FROM *REMINISCENCES OF MY LIFE IN CAMP*

SUSIE KING TAYLOR

About this time I had been reading so much about the "Yankees" I was very anxious to see them. The whites would tell their colored people not to go to the Yankees, for they would harness them to carts and make them pull the carts around, in place of horses. I asked grandmother, one day, if this was true. She replied, "Certainly not!" that the white people did not want slaves to go over to the Yankees, and told them these things to frighten them. "Don't you see those signs pasted about the streets? one reading, 'I am a rattlesnake; if you touch me I will strike!' Another reads, 'I am a wild cat! Beware,' etc. These are warnings to the North; so don't mind what the white people say." I wanted to see these wonderful "Yankees" so much, as I heard my parents say the Yankee was going to set all the slaves free. Oh, how those people prayed for freedom! I remember, one night, my grandmother went out into the suburbs of the city to a church meeting, and they were fervently singing this old hymn,—

> "Yes, we all shall be free,
> Yes, we all shall be free,
> Yes, we all shall be free,
> When the Lord shall appear,"—

when the police came in and arrested all who were there, saying they were planning freedom, and sang "the Lord," in place of "Yankee," to blind any one who might be listening. Grandmother never forgot that night, although she did not stay in the guard-house, as she sent to her guardian, who came at once for her; but this was the last meeting she ever attended out of the city proper.

From Susie King Taylor, *Reminiscences of My Life in Camp* (Boston: Susie King Taylor, 1902), 7–9.

On April 1,1862, about the time the Union soldiers were firing on Fort Pulaski, I was sent out into the country to my mother. I remember what a roar and din the guns made. They jarred the earth for miles. The fort was at last taken by them. Two days after the taking of Fort Pulaski, my uncle took his family of seven and myself to St. Catherine Island. We landed under the protection of the Union fleet, and remained there two weeks, when about thirty of us were taken aboard the gunboat P——, to be transferred to St. Simon's Island; and at last, to my unbounded joy, I saw the "Yankee."

DRAWING CONCLUSIONS:

1. What does Taylor's memoir reveal about the factors that led many southern slaves to leave their homes for Union lines in the period before the Emancipation Proclamation?

3.7   JOHN BOSTON TO ELIZABETH BOSTON (JANUARY 12, 1862)

John Boston was a runaway slave from Maryland who took refuge with a Union regiment. In this January 1862 letter to his with Elizabeth, Boston shares his current situation and his hopes for the future. Very few slaves were literate (teaching a slave to read and write was generally barred by law in southern states), so this letter provides a rare glimpse into the thoughts and feelings of a fugitive slave in the early stage of the war in his own words. Keep in mind that, at the time Boston wrote this letter he was, under federal law, still considered legally enslaved.

GUIDING QUESTIONS:

1. How does Boston describe his current situation and his hopes for the future?
2. Under federal law, Boston was still considered a slave at the time he wrote this letter. Why then do you think he describes himself as a "free man"?

Upton Hill [Va.] January the 12th 1862

My Dear Wife it is with grate joy I take this time to let you know Whare I am i am now in Safety in the 14th Regiment of Brooklyn this Day i can Adress you thank god as a free man I had a little truble in giting away But as the lord led the Children of Isrel to the land of Canon So he led me to a land Whare fredom Will rain in spite Of earth and hell Dear you must make your Self content i am free from al the Slavers Lash and as you have chose the Wise plan Of Serving the lord i hope you Will pray Much and i Will try by the help of god to Serv him With all my hart I am With a very nice man and have All that hart Can Wish But My Dear I Cant express my grate desire that i Have to See you i trust the time Will Come When We Shal meet again And if We dont met on earth We Will Meet in heven Whare Jesus ranes Dear Elizabeth tell Mrs Own[ees] That i trust that She Will Continue Her kindness to you and that god Will Bless her on earth and Save her In grate eternity My Acomplements to Mrs Owens and her Children may They Prosper through life I never Shall forgit her kindness to me Dear Wife i must Close rest yourself Contented i am free i Want you to rite To me Soon as you Can Without Delay Direct your letter to the 14th Reigment New York State militia Uptons Hill Virginea In Care of Mr Cranford Comary Write my Dear Soon As you C Your Affectionate Husban Kiss Daniel For me

John Boston

Give my love to Father and Mother

DRAWING CONCLUSIONS:

1. What does this letter reveal about how slaves, at least in certain cases, viewed the issues at stake in the Civil War in the period before the Emancipation Proclamation?

From Ira Berlin et al., eds., *Free At Last: A Documentary History of Slavery, Freedom, and the Civil War* (New York: The New Press, 1992), 45–46.

3.8 EXCHANGE BETWEEN GENERAL ORMSBY M. MITCHEL AND EDWIN M. STANTON (MAY 1862)

In the spring of 1862, federal troops under the command of General Ormsby M. Mitchel pushed into northern Alabama. In this letter, Mitchel informs Secretary of War Edwin M. Stanton of the important assistance he had received from the slave population residing in the area, and he asks Stanton for permission to provide protection to those who had assisted the Union troops. In this letter, we can see how the aid that southern slaves provided to the Union war effort helped to shape federal policy toward slavery.

GUIDING QUESTIONS:

1. What assistance does Mitchel say the slaves of northern Alabama provided to him and his forces?
2. Why does Mitchel say it is vital that those who assisted him be protected?
3. What is Stanton's reply to Mitchel's request? What reasons does he give for this reply?

ORMSBY M. MITCHEL TO EDWIN M. STANTON

HUNTSVILLE [ALA.] MAY 4 1862

I have this day written you fully embracing three topics of great importance. The absolute necessity of protecting slaves who furnish us valuable information—the fact that I am left with out the command of my line of communications and the importance of holding Alabama north of the Tennessee. I have promised protection to the slaves who have given me valuable assistance and information. My River front is 120 miles long and if the Government disapprove what I have done I must receive heavy re enforcements or abandon my position. With the assistance of the Negroes in watching the River I feel my self sufficiently strong to defy the enemy.

O. M. Mitchel

EDWIN M. STANTON TO ORMSBY M. MITCHEL

WASHINGTON [DC] 5 MAY 1862

General O M Mitchel, Your Telegram of the 3d and 4th have been received No General in the field has deserved better of his Government than yourself and the department rejoices to award credit to one who merits it so well. The Department is advised of nothing that you have done but what it has approved The assistance of slaves is an element of military strength which under proper regulations you are fully justified in employing for your security and the success of your operations. It has been freely employed by the enemy: and to abstain from its use when it can be employed with military advantage would be a failure to employ means to suppress the Rebellion and retrieve the authority of the Government. Protection to those who furnish information or other assistance is a high Duty.

Edwin M Stanton

DRAWING CONCLUSIONS:

1. What does this exchange reveal about the factors shaping federal policy toward slaves and slavery in the period prior to the Emancipation Proclamation?

From Ira Berlin et al., eds., *Free At Last: A Documentary History of Slavery, Freedom, and the Civil War* (New York: The New Press, 1992), 30.

3.9 AN ACT TO MAKE AN ADDITIONAL ARTICLE OF WAR (MARCH 13, 1862)

The First Confiscation Act declared slaves employed in service of the rebellion to be free. It provided Union military officers with no guidance, however, regarding the stance to adopt toward the thousands of other slaves who escaped or came within to Union lines. Some officers welcomed and protected runaway slaves. Others turned them away from federal encampments. Some returned runaway slaves to masters who demanded their return. Others did not. In March 1862, the Congress resolved the issue of military policy toward escaped slaves in "An Act to Make an Additional Article of War."

GUIDING QUESTIONS:

1. In this piece of legislation, what did the Congress declare military policy toward escaped slaves to be?

AN ACT TO MAKE AN ADDITIONAL ARTICLE OF WAR

MARCH 13, 1862

Be it enacted by the Senate and House of Representatives of the United States of America in Congress assembled, That hereafter the following shall be promulgated as an additional article of war for the government of the army of the United States, and shall be obeyed and observed as such:

Article—. All officers or persons in the military or naval service of the United States are prohibited from employing any of the forces under their respective commands for the purpose of returning fugitives from service or labor, who may have escaped from any persons to whom such service or labor is claimed to be due, and any officer who shall be found guilty by a court-martial of violating this article shall be dismissed from the service.

Sec. 2. *And be it further enacted*, That this act shall take effect from and after its passage.

Approved, March 13, 1862.

DRAWING CONCLUSIONS:

1. What does this piece of legislation reveal about the impact of runaway slaves on federal policymakers?

From *The Statutes at Large, Treaties, and Proclamations of the United States of America*, 37th Congress, 2nd Session, 354.

FRÉMONT'S PROCLAMATION

While the Lincoln administration continued to reassure southern slave owners that it had no intention to interfere with the institution of slavery, some Union military officers began to advocate a bolder anti-slavery stand. Among those was General John C. Frémont, the commander of Union forces in the state of Missouri. Missouri, a slave state deeply divided into pro-Confederate and pro-Union factions, saw some of the fiercest fighting in the early months of the war. In August 1861, Frémont issued a military proclamation declaring martial law in the state, allowing for the execution of armed rebels, and declaring all slaves owned by those actively in support of the rebellion to be free.

4.1 FRÉMONT'S PROCLAMATION AND LINCOLN'S RESPONSE (AUGUST–SEPTEMBER 1861)

President Lincoln quickly overruled Frémont's proclamation. This document includes both Frémont's proclamation itself and Lincoln's response.

GUIDING QUESTIONS:

1. What clues does Frémont's proclamation provide regarding his motives for declaring the slaves of those in the support of the rebellion to be free?
2. What reasons does President Lincoln give for overruling Frémont's emancipation proclamation?

FRÉMONT'S PROCLAMATION

PROCLAMATION

HEADQUARTERS WESTERN DEPARTMENT, SAINT LOUIS, AUGUST 30, 1861.

Circumstances, in my judgment, of sufficient urgency render it necessary that the commanding general of this department should assume the administrative powers of the State. Its disorganized condition, the helplessness of the civil authority, the total insecurity of life, and the devastation of property by bands of murderers and marauders, who infest nearly every county of the State, and avail themselves of the public misfortunes and the vicinity of a hostile force to gratify private and neighborhood vengeance, and who find an enemy wherever they find plunder, finally demand the severest measures to repress the daily-increasing crimes and outrages which are driving off the inhabitants and ruining the State.

In this condition the public safety and the success of our arms require unity of purpose, without let or hinderance to the prompt administration of affairs. In order, therefore, to suppress disorder, to maintain as far as now practicable the public peace, and to give security and protection to the persons and property of loyal citizens, I do hereby extend and declare established martial law throughout the State of Missouri.

The lines of the army of occupation in this State are for the present declared to extend from Leavenworth, by way of the posts of Jefferson City, Rolla, and Ironton, to Cape Girardeau, on the Mississippi River.

All persons who shall be taken with arms in their hands within these lines shall be tried by court-martial, and if found guilty will be shot.

The property, real and personal, of all persons in the State of Missouri who shall take up arms against the United States, or who shall be directly proven to have taken an active part with their enemies in the field, is declared to be confiscated to the public use, and their slaves, if any they have, are hereby declared freemen.

All persons who shall be proven to have destroyed, after the publication of this order, railroad tracks, bridges, or telegraphs shall suffer the extreme penalty of the law.

From *The War of the Rebellion: A Compilation of the Official Records of the Union and Confederate Armies*, Series 1, Volume 3, 466–467.

All persons engaged in treasonable correspondence, in giving or procuring aid to the enemies of the United States, in fomenting tumults, in disturbing the public tranquillity by creating and circulating false reports or incendiary documents, are in their own interests warned that they are exposing themselves to sudden and severe punishment.

All persons who have been led away from their allegiance are required to return to their homes forthwith. Any such absence, without sufficient cause, will be held to be presumptive evidence against them.

The object of this declaration is to place in the hands of the military authorities the power to give instantaneous effect to existing laws, and to supply such deficiencies as the conditions of war demand. But this is not intended to suspend the ordinary tribunals of the country, where the law will be administered by the civil officers in the usual manner, and with their customary authority, while the same can be peaceably exercised.

The commanding general will labor vigilantly for the public welfare, and in his efforts for their safety hopes to obtain not only the acquiescence but the active support of the loyal people of the country.

J. C. FREMONT,
Major-General, Commanding.

LINCOLN TO JOHN C. FRÉMONT

PRIVATE AND CONFIDENTIAL. MAJOR GENERAL FREMONT: WASHINGTON D.C. SEPT. 2, 1861.

My dear Sir: Two points in your proclamation of August 30th give me some anxiety. First, should you shoot a man, according to the proclamation, the Confederates would very certainly shoot our best man in their hands in retaliation; and so, man for man, indefinitely. It is therefore my order that you allow no man to be shot, under the proclamation, without first having my approbation or consent.

Secondly, I think there is great danger that the closing paragraph, in relation to the confiscation of property, and the liberating slaves of traiterous owners, will alarm our Southern Union friends, and turn them against us—perhaps ruin our rather fair prospect for Kentucky. Allow me therefore to ask, that you will as of your own motion, modify that paragraph so as to conform to the first and fourth sections of the act of Congress, entitled, "An act to confiscate property used for insurrectionary purposes," approved August 6th, 1861, and a copy of which act I herewith send you. This letter is written in a spirit of caution and not of censure.

I send it by a special messenger, in order that it may certainly and speedily reach you. Yours very truly
A. LINCOLN

DRAWING CONCLUSIONS:

1. What does the exchange between Lincoln and Frémont reveal about the factors Union military officers and policymakers had to consider when responding to the issue of slavery in the early stages of the war?
2. What does Lincoln's response to Frémont reveal about Lincoln's political priorities in the early stages of the war?

From Roy P. Basler, ed., *The Collected Works of Abraham Lincoln*, vol. 4 (New Brunswick, NJ: Rutgers University Press, 1953), 506.

4.2   LINCOLN TO ORVILLE H. BROWNING (SEPTEMBER 22, 1861)

Abolitionists and their sympathizers in the Congress were sharply critical of Lincoln for overturning Frémont's proclamation. In this letter to Illinois Senator Orville H. Browning, Lincoln's closest personal friend in the Congress, Lincoln defends his decision.

GUIDING QUESTIONS:

1. What reasons does Lincoln give for overturning Frémont's proclamation?

LINCOLN TO ORVILLE H. BROWNING

PRIVATE & CONFIDENTIAL.
HON. O. H. BROWNING EXECUTIVE
MANSION WASHINGTON
SEPT 22D 1861.

My dear Sir

Yours of the 17th is just received; and coming from you, I confess it astonishes me. That you should object to my adhering to a law, which you had assisted in making, and presenting to me, less than a month before, is odd enough. But this is a very small part. Genl. Fremont's proclamation, as to confiscation of property, and the liberation of slaves, is purely political, and not within the range of military law, or necessity. If a commanding General finds a necessity to seize the farm of a private owner, for a pasture, an encampment, or a fortification, he has the right to do so, and to so hold it, as long as the necessity lasts; and this is within military law, because within military necessity. But to say the farm shall no longer belong to the owner, or his heirs forever; and this as well when the farm is not needed for military purposes as when it is, is purely political, without the savor of military law about it. And the same is true of slaves. If the General needs them, he can seize them, and use them; but when the need is past, it is not for him to fix their permanent future condition. That must be settled according to laws made by law-makers, and not by military proclamations. The proclamation in the point in question, is simply "dictatorship." It assumes that the general may do anything he pleases—confiscate the lands and free the slaves of loyal people, as well as of disloyal ones. And going the whole figure I have no doubt would be more popular with some thoughtless people, than that which has been done! But I cannot assume this reckless position; nor allow others to assume it on my responsibility. You speak of it as being the only means of saving the government. On the contrary it is itself the surrender of the government. Can it be pretended that it is any longer the government of the U.S.—any government of Constitution and laws,—wherein a General, or a President, may make permanent rules of property by proclamation?

I do not say Congress might not with propriety pass a law, on the point, just such as General Fremont proclaimed. I do not say I might not, as a member of Congress, vote for it. What I object to, is, that I as President, shall expressly or impliedly seize and exercise the permanent legislative functions of the government.

So much as to principle. Now as to policy. No doubt the thing was popular in some quarters, and would have been more so if it had been a general declaration of emancipation. The Kentucky Legislature would not budge till that proclamation was modified; and Gen. Anderson telegraphed me that on the

From Roy P. Basler, ed., *The Collected Works of Abraham Lincoln*, vol. 4 (New Brunswick, NJ: Rutgers University Press, 1953), 531–533.

news of Gen. Fremont having actually issued deeds of manumission, a whole company of our Volunteers threw down their arms and disbanded. I was so assured, as to think it probable, that the very arms we had furnished Kentucky would be turned against us. I think to lose Kentucky is nearly the same as to lose the whole game. Kentucky gone, we can not hold Missouri, nor, as I think, Maryland. These all against us, and the job on our hands is too large for us. We would as well consent to separation at once, including the surrender of this capitol. On the contrary, if you will give up your restlessness for new positions, and back me manfully on the grounds upon which you and other kind friends gave me the election, and have approved in my public documents, we shall go through triumphantly.

You must not understand I took my course on the proclamation because of Kentucky. I took the same ground in a private letter to General Fremont before I heard from Kentucky.

You think I am inconsistent because I did not also forbid Gen. Fremont to shoot men under the proclamation. I understand that part to be within military law; but I also think, and so privately wrote Gen. Fremont, that it is impolitic in this, that our adversaries have the power, and will certainly exercise it, to shoot as many of our men as we shoot of theirs. I did not say this in the public letter, because it is a subject I prefer not to discuss in the hearing of our enemies.

There has been no thought of removing Gen. Fremont on any ground connected with his proclamation; and if there has been any wish for his removal on any ground, our mutual friend Sam. Glover can probably tell you what it was. I hope no real necessity for it exists on any ground.

Suppose you write to Hurlbut and get him to resign. Your friend as ever A. LINCOLN

DRAWING CONCLUSIONS:

1. What does this letter reveal about the reasons that Lincoln was reluctant to act against slavery in the early stages of the Civil War?

4.3 FREDERICK DOUGLASS, "GENERAL FRÉMONT'S PROCLAMATION TO THE REBELS OF MISSOURI" (OCTOBER 1861)

Frémont's proclamation, and Lincoln's response, captured the attention of the nation. Abolitionists were thrilled by the general's bold action and disappointed in the President's response. In this article, black abolitionist leader Frederick Douglass provides his commentary on the controversy. The article is taken from the October 1861 issue of *Douglass' Monthly*, an anti-slavery magazine published and edited by Douglass. The article provides a sense of how slavery's future had become an issue on northern politics well before Lincoln issued his Preliminary Emancipation Proclamation in the fall of 1862.

GUIDING QUESTIONS:

1. Why does Douglass consider Frémont's proclamation to be of such great importance?
2. What conclusions does Douglass draw from Lincoln's response to the proclamation?

GENERAL FREMONT'S PROCLAMATION TO THE REBELS OF MISSOURI

Considering the position of the State of Missouri, the divided state of its people between loyalty and treason, the geographical relation of the State to its sisters of the free North and the slave South, and the persistent and desperate efforts of the rebels to drive the State out of the Union, and the necessity for prompt and energetic action on the part of the Government, the public have generally concurred in the judgement that General Fremont is the right man in the right place, and that his now celebrated Proclamation is by far the most important and salutary measure which has thus far emanated from any General during the whole tedious progress of the war. It impressed the country with the idea that the hour, the place and the man were equally well filled. The Proclamation, which we publish elsewhere in our present number, will be seen to be singular only in one of its features; but that particular one happens to be the radical and distinctive feature of the rebellion itself.

It takes the bull by the horns at once, and declares the slaves of all duly convicted traitors in the State of Missouri, *"free men."* They are not only confiscated property, but *liberated men*.

The paragraph devoted to this subject is remarkably short and simple, but, we think, strong enough to convulse a continent. It caused a shout of joy to burst from the hearts of the genuine lovers of the Union and the rights of mankind, while it carried terror and dismay into the ranks of rebellion. The admission was general and hearty, that the celebrated pathfinder, in this simple document, had successfully marked out, to a bewildered and distracted nation, the true and only wise path out of its troubles and difficulties.

For many days after the publication of Fremont's Proclamation, the deepest anxiety existed throughout the country to learn whether that remarkable and startling document was the utterance of the Major-General, or that of the Cabinet at Washington—whether, if only from the former, the

From *The Life and Writings of Frederick Douglass*, vol. 3 (New York: International Publishers, 1975), 159–162.

President would approve it or condemn it? Those who had confidence in the anti-slavery character and disposition of the Administration, unhesitatingly ascribed it to the wisdom, earnestness and courage that controls at Washington. While others, entertaining opposite impressions, openly predicted, what has since transpired, a pointed disapproval by the President of the main feature of Fremont's Proclamation. The suspense was truly painful, and attested the vast importance attached by the public to the measure. The action of Fremont was the hinge, the pivot upon which the character of the war was to turn. It was whether the war should be waged against traitors only by the cunning technicalities of the crafty lawyer, or by the cannon and courage of the determined warrior.

Unhappily, as we think, for the country and for humanity, the lawyer has prevailed over the warrior. The President, of whom we would gladly speak naught but good, has interposed, most unseasonably, by his Presidential authority, and placed a tame and worthless statute between the rebels and the merited chastisement which a brave and generous General had wisely prepared himself to inflict upon them. Many blunders have been committed by the Government at Washington during the war, but this, we think, is the hugest of them all. The Government should have thanked their wise and intrepid General for furnishing them an opportunity to convince the country and the world of their earnestness, that they have no terms for traitors; that with them the heaviest blow is the wisest and best blow; and that the rebels must be put down at all hazards, and in the most summary and exemplary way. But, poor souls! instead of standing by the General, and approving his energetic conduct, they have humbled and crippled him in the presence of his enemies. The President interposes to cheapen the price of rebellion, and to let the rebels off on the easier terms than that proposed by his faithful General.

We know not upon what maxim of political wisdom the Government has acted in this matter. The Cabinet is composed of reputed wise men, and the President is respected as honest and humane. But this policy is plainly one which can only dishearten the friends of the Government and strengthen its enemies. The *Times* newspaper of New York defends the anti-Fremont policy, by alleging that the rigor of that policy would drive the loyal slaveholders in Kentucky and Tennessee into the arms of the rebels. This assumption would have some weight did Fremont's Proclamation propose (as it does not) the liberation of the slaves of loyal masters. It strikes only at slaveholding rebels; and to suppose that loyal masters would be driven into disloyalty by the well-merited chastisement of slaveholding rebels, implies that, after all, there is a stronger bond existing between these loyal slaveholders and the slaveholding rebels, than subsists between the former and the Government. Taking this admission to be true, and what is the friendship of these so-called loyal slaveholders worth? The open hostility of these so-called loyal slaveholders is incomparably to be preferred to their friendship. They are far more easily dealt with and disposed of as enemies than as allies. From the beginning, these Border Slave States have been the mill-stone about the neck of the Government, and their so-called loyalty has been the very best shield to the treason of the cotton States.

President Lincoln says in his letter to Gen. Fremont, that he accords with the general character of his Proclamation. One clause of it only is marked for disapproval, and that is the emancipating clause. Now mark! The Proclamation imposes that most dreaded of all descriptions of law, (except mob law,) martial law upon Missouri. The President approves that. The Proclamation proposes the confiscation of the property of the rebels. The President approves that. The Proclamation proposes that convicted rebels, within certain defined lines, *shall be shot*. The President approves that. The Proclamation proposes that the slaves of duly convicted traitors shall be liberated and treated as *free men.*—Here's the rub; the President does not approve that. Martial law, shooting, confiscation, with all their aggravation, are assented to; but liberation and freedom to the slave are vetoed by the President of the United States. The weakness, imbecility and absurdity of this policy are sufficiently manifest without a single word of comment.

It still remains to be seem what course Gen. Fremont will take in view of the restrictions which have thus been thrown around him—whether he will continue in his command, resign, or be dismissed. One thing, however, seems certain: the People confide both in the patriotism and in the ability of Frémont, and would regard the loss of that able man to the service of the country as little less disastrous and distressing than the defeat of the Government forces by the rebels at Bull Run; and yet, considering the nature of the humiliation sought to be imposed upon the young and spirited General, his resignation would not be a surprise, though a deep regret to the country.

DRAWING CONCLUSIONS

1. What can we learn from this document about the impact in the North of Frémont's proclamation and Lincoln's response?

GRADUAL EMANCIPATION

Although Lincoln continued to resist calls for broad emancipation measures, by the end of 1861, he had begun to gently suggest that individual slave states (particularly those that had rejected secession) consider the gradual abolition of slavery within their borders with compensation for slave owners. Lincoln's advocacy for gradual emancipation marked an important evolution in his stance on the slavery question, although the exact motives for this shift remain somewhat unclear.

5.1   ABRAHAM LINCOLN, "ANNUAL MESSAGE TO CONGRESS" (DECEMBER 3, 1861)

Lincoln's first public mention as president of gradual emancipation came in his December 1861 annual message to Congress. In this excerpt from the annual message, note how he links gradual emancipation to the "contraband" issue and links both issues to a proposal to encourage the emigration (or "colonization") of freed slaves outside the United States.

GUIDING QUESTIONS:

1. How does Lincoln introduce the idea of gradual emancipation in his annual message? What does he say the federal government could do to encourage it?
2. What does Lincoln suggest could become of former slaves who are freed either through confiscation or through gradual emancipation at the state level?
3. Toward the end of the message, Lincoln responds to those calling for more sweeping anti-slavery measures. What does Lincoln say to those who advocating bold steps toward emancipation?

LINCOLN'S ANNUAL MESSAGE TO CONGRESS

DECEMBER 3, 1861

Under and by virtue of the act of Congress en-
. . . titled "An act to confiscate property used for
insurrectionary purposes," approved August, 6, 1861,
the legal claims of certain persons to the labor and
service of certain other persons have become forfeited;
and numbers of the latter, thus liberated, are already
dependent on the United States, and must be provided
for in some way. Besides this, it is not impossible
that some of the States will pass similar enactments
for their own benefit respectively, and by operation
of which persons of the same class will be thrown
upon them for disposal. In such case I recommend
that Congress provide for accepting such persons from
such States, according to some mode of valuation, in
lieu, pro tanto, of direct taxes, or upon some other
plan to be agreed on with such States respectively;
that such persons, on such acceptance by the general
government, be at once deemed free; and that, in
any event, steps be taken for colonizing both classes,
(or the one first mentioned, if the other shall not be
brought into existence,) at some place, or places, in
a climate congenial to them. It might be well to consider, too,—whether the free colored people already
in the United States could not, so far as individuals
may desire, be included in such colonization.

To carry out the plan of colonization may involve
the acquiring of territory, and also the appropriation
of money beyond that to be expended in the territorial acquisition. Having practiced the acquisition of
territory for nearly sixty years, the question of constitutional power to do so is no longer an open one with
us. The power was questioned at first by Mr. Jefferson,
who, however, in the purchase of Louisiana, yielded
his scruples on the plea of great expediency. If it be
said that the only legitimate object of acquiring territory is to furnish homes for white men, this measure

From Roy P. Basler, ed., *The Collected Works of Abraham Lincoln*, vol. 5 (New Brunswick, NJ: Rutgers University Press, 1953), 48–49.

effects that object; for the emigration of colored men leaves additional room for white men remaining or coming here. Mr. Jefferson, however, placed the importance of procuring Louisiana more on political and commercial grounds than on providing room for population.

On this whole proposition,—including the appropriation of money with the acquisition of territory, does not the expediency amount to absolute necessity—that, without which the government itself cannot be perpetuated? The war continues. In considering the policy to be adopted for suppressing the insurrection, I have been anxious and careful that the inevitable conflict for this purpose shall not degenerate into a violent and remorseless revolutionary struggle. I have, therefore, in every case, thought it proper to keep the integrity of the Union prominent as the primary object of the contest on our part, leaving all questions which are not of vital military importance to the more deliberate action of the legislature.

In the exercise of my best discretion I have adhered to the blockade of the ports held by the insurgents, instead of putting in force, by proclamation, the law of Congress enacted at the late session, for closing those ports.

So, also, obeying the dictates of prudence, as well as the obligations of law, instead of transcending, I have adhered to the act of Congress to confiscate property used for insurrectionary purposes. If a new law upon the same subject shall be proposed, its propriety will be duly considered.

The Union must be preserved, and hence, all indispensable means must be employed. We should not be in haste to determine that radical and extreme measures, which may reach the loyal as well as the disloyal, are indispensable. . . .

DRAWING CONCLUSIONS:

1. How would you summarize Lincoln's position on the slavery issue as presented in the December 1861 annual message?

2. What does the message suggest about Lincoln's views on issues of race at the time?

5.2   ABRAHAM LINCOLN, "MESSAGE TO CONGRESS" (MARCH 6, 1862)

In March of 1862, Lincoln sent a message to Congress urging it to take practical steps to encourage slave states to adopt gradual emancipation plans. The message is presented here in full.

GUIDING QUESTIONS:

1. What is Lincoln asking Congress to do to encourage gradual emancipation at the state level?
2. What reasons does Lincoln give for encouraging gradual emancipation at the state level?
3. Toward the end of the message, Lincoln writes, "If, however, resistance continues, the war must also continue; and it is impossible to foresee all the incidents, which may attend and all the ruin which may follow it. Such as may seem indispensable, or may obviously promise great efficiency towards ending the struggle, must and will come." What does he mean by this?

LINCOLN'S MESSAGE TO CONGRESS

MARCH 6, 1862

Fellow-citizens of the Senate, and House of Representatives,

I recommend the adoption of a Joint Resolution by your honorable bodies which shall be substantially as follows:

"Resolved that the United States ought to co-operate with any state which may adopt gradual abolishment of slavery, giving to such state pecuniary aid, to be used by such state in it's discretion, to compensate for the inconveniences public and private, produced by such change of system."

If the proposition contained in the resolution does not meet the approval of Congress and the country, there is the end; but if it does command such approval, I deem it of importance that the states and people immediately interested, should be at once distinctly notified of the fact, so that they may begin to consider whether to accept or reject it. The federal government would find its highest interest in such a measure, as one of the most efficient means of self-preservation. The leaders of the existing insurrection entertain the hope that this government will ultimately be forced to acknowledge the independence of some part of the disaffected region, and that all the slave states North of such part will then say "the Union, for which we have struggled, being already gone, we now choose to go with the Southern section." To deprive them of this hope, substantially ends the rebellion; and the initiation of emancipation completely deprives them of it, as to all the states initiating it. The point is not that all the states tolerating slavery would very soon, if at all, initiate emancipation; but that, while the offer is equally made to all, the more Northern shall, by such initiation, make it certain to the more Southern, that in no event, will the former ever join the latter, in their proposed confederacy. I say "initiation" because, in my judgment, gradual, and not sudden emancipation, is better for all. In the mere financial, or pecuniary view, any member of Congress, with the census-tables and

From Roy P. Basler, ed., *The Collected Works of Abraham Lincoln*, vol. 5 (New Brunswick, NJ: Rutgers University Press, 1953), 144–146.

Treasury-reports before him, can readily see for him-self how very soon the current expenditures of this war would purchase, at fair valuation, all the slaves in any named State. Such a proposition, on the part of the general government, sets up no claim of a right, by federal authority, to interfere with slavery within state limits, referring, as it does, the absolute control of the subject, in each case, to the state and it's people, immediately interested. It is proposed as a matter of perfectly free choice with them.

In the annual message last December, I thought fit to say "The Union must be preserved; and hence all indispensable means must be employed." I said this, not hastily, but deliberately. War has been made, and continues to be, an indispensable means to this end. A practical re-acknowledgement of the national authority would render the war unnecessary, and it would at once cease. If, however, resistance continues, the war must also continue; and it is impossible to foresee all the incidents, which may attend and all the ruin which may follow it. Such as may seem indispensable, or may obviously promise great efficiency towards ending the struggle, must and will come.

The proposition now made, though an offer only, I hope it may be esteemed no offence to ask whether the pecuniary consideration tendered would not be of more value to the States and private persons concerned, than are the institution, and property in it, in the present aspect of affairs.

While it is true that the adoption of the proposed resolution would be merely initiatory, and not within itself a practical measure, it is recommended in the hope that it would soon lead to important practical results. In full view of my great responsibility to my God, and to my country, I earnestly beg the attention of Congress and the people to the subject. ABRAHAM LINCOLN

March 6. 1862.

DRAWING CONCLUSIONS:

1. How would you summarize Lincoln's position on the issue of slavery as presented in the March 1862 message to Congress?
2. How, if at all, had Lincoln's position or tone on the slavery issue evolved between the December 1861 annual message and the March 1862 message?

5.3   J. W. CRISFIELD, "MEMORANDUM OF AN INTERVIEW BETWEEN THE PRESIDENT AND SOME BORDER SLAVE-STATE REPRESENTATIVES" (MARCH 10, 1862)

Shortly after Lincoln sent the message to Congress advocating gradual emancipation, the President invited representatives of the border slave states to the White House to discuss his proposal. This document, authored by Maryland Congressman John W. Crisfield, is a summary of the conversation between Lincoln and the border state representatives. The conversation began with Lincoln making the case for his proposal followed by questions and an exchange of views between Lincoln as his guests. Note carefully how the argument that Lincoln makes for gradual emancipation in the privacy of the White House differs in significant ways from the case he made in his message to Congress, which was a public document. In the conversation, Lincoln makes reference to the *New York Tribune* and the "Greely faction." Horace Greeley, editor of the *New York Tribune*, was one of the most influential voices pressuring Lincoln to take bolder steps against the institution of slavery.

GUIDING QUESTIONS:

1. What reasons does Lincoln give for his gradual emancipation proposal? How do the reasons given in this private conversation differ from those he gave in his message to Congress?
2. What concerns do the border state representatives raise about Lincoln's proposal? How does Lincoln respond to these concerns?
3. How, in particular, does Lincoln respond to concerns that, if the gradual emancipation proposal is rejected, he might pursue bolder steps against slavery?

MEMORANDUM OF AN INTERVIEW BETWEEN THE PRESIDENT AND SOME BORDER SLAVE-STATE REPRESENTATIVES, BY HON. J.W. CRISFIELD

"DEAR SIR:—I called, at the request of the President, to ask you to come to the White House to-morrow morning, at nine o'clock, and bring such of your colleagues as are in town."

WASHINGTON, March 10, 1862.

Yesterday, on my return from church, I found Mr. Postmaster-General Blair in my room, writing the above note, which he immediately suspended, and verbally communicated the President's invitation, and stated that the President's purpose was to have some conversation with the delegations of Kentucky, Missouri, Maryland, Virginia, and Delaware, in explanation of his message of the 6th instant.

This morning these delegations, or such of them as were in town, assembled at the White House at the appointed time, and after some little delay were admitted to an audience. Mr. Leary and myself were the only members from Maryland present, and, I think, were the only members of the delegation at that time in the city. I know that Mr. Pearoe, of the Senate, and Messrs. Webster and Calvert, of the House, were absent.

From Arthur Brooks Lapsley's *The Writings of Abraham Lincoln*, vol. 5 (New York: G.P. Putnam's Sons, 1906), 446–452.

After the usual salutations, and we were seated, the President said, in substance, that he had invited us to meet him to have some conversation with us in explanation of his message of the 6th; that since he had sent it in several of the gentlemen then present had visited him, but had avoided any allusion to the message, and he therefore inferred that the import of the message had been misunderstood, and was regarded as inimical to the interests we represented; and he had resolved he would talk with us, and disabuse our minds of that erroneous opinion.

The President then disclaimed any intent to injure the interests or wound the sensibilities of the slave States. On the contrary, his purpose was to protect the one and respect the other; that we were engaged in a terrible, wasting, and tedious war; immense armies were in the field, and must continue in the field as long as the war lasts; that these armies must, of necessity, be brought into contact with slaves in the States we represented and in other States as they advanced; that slaves would come to the camps, and continual irritation was kept up; that he was constantly annoyed by conflicting and antagonistic complaints: on the one side a certain class complained if the slave was not protected by the army; persons were frequently found who, participating in these views, acted in a way unfriendly to the slaveholder; on the other hand, slaveholders complained that their rights were interfered with, their slaves induced to abscond and protected within the lines; these complaints were numerous, loud and deep; were a serious annoyance to him and embarrassing to the progress of the war; that it kept alive a spirit hostile to the government in the States we represented; strengthened the hopes of the Confederates that at some day the border States would unite with them, and thus tend to prolong the war; and he was of opinion, if this resolution should be adopted by Congress and accepted by our States, these causes of irritation and these hopes would be removed, and more would be accomplished toward shortening the war than could be hoped from the greatest victory achieved by Union armies; that he made this proposition in good faith, and desired it to be accepted, if at all, voluntarily, and in the same patriotic spirit in which it was made; that emancipation was a subject exclusively under the control of the States, and must be adopted or rejected by each for itself; that he did not claim nor had this government any right to coerce them for that purpose; that such was no part of his purpose in making this proposition, and he wished it to be clearly understood; that he did not expect us there to be prepared to give him an answer, but he hoped we would take the subject into serious consideration, confer with one another, and then take such course as we felt our duty and the interests of our constituents required of us.

Mr. Noell, of Missouri, said that in his State slavery was not considered a permanent institution; that natural causes were there in operation which would at no distant day extinguish it, and he did not think that this proposition was necessary for that; and, besides that, he and his friends felt solicitous as to the message on account of the different constructions which the resolution and message had received. The New York Tribune was for it, and understood it to mean that we must accept gradual emancipation according to the plan suggested, or get something worse.

The President replied that he must not be expected to quarrel with the New York Tribune before the right time; he hoped never to have to do it; he would not anticipate events. In respect to emancipation in Missouri, he said that what had been observed by Mr. Noell was probably true, but the operation of these natural causes had not prevented the irritating conduct to which he had referred, or destroyed the hopes of the Confederates that Missouri would at some time merge herself alongside of them, which, in his judgment, the passage of this resolution by Congress and its acceptance by Missouri would accomplish.

Mr. Crisfield, of Maryland, asked what would be the effect of the refusal of the State to accept this proposal, and he desired to know if the President looked to any policy beyond the acceptance or rejection of this scheme.

The President replied that he had no designs beyond the actions of the States on this particular subject. He should lament their refusal to accept it, but he had no designs beyond their refusal of it.

Mr. Menzies, of Kentucky, inquired if the President thought there was any power except in the States themselves to carry out his scheme of emancipation.

The President replied that he thought there could not be. He then went off into a course of remarks not qualifying the foregoing declaration nor material to be repeated to a just understanding of his meaning.

Mr. Crisfield said he did not think the people of Maryland looked upon slavery as a permanent institution; and he did not know that they would be very reluctant to give it up if provision was made to meet the loss and they could be rid of the race; but they did not like to be coerced into emancipation, either by the direct action of the government or by indirection, as through the emancipation of slaves in this District, or the confiscation of Southern property as now threatened; and he thought before they would consent to consider this proposition they would require to be informed on these points. The President replied that, unless he was expelled by the act of God or the Confederate armies he should occupy that house for three years; and as long as he remained there Maryland had nothing to fear either for her institutions or her interests on the points referred to.

Mr. Crisfield immediately added: "Mr. President, if what you now say could be heard by the people of Maryland, they would consider your proposition with a much better feeling than I fear without it they will be inclined to do."

The President: "That [meaning a publication of what he said] will not do; it would force me into a quarrel before the proper time"; and, again intimating, as he had before done, that a quarrel with the "Greeley faction" was impending, he said he did not wish to encounter it before the proper time, nor at all if it could be avoided.

Governor Wickliffe, of Kentucky, then asked him respecting the constitutionality of his scheme.

The President replied: "As you may suppose, I have considered that; and the proposition now submitted does not encounter any constitutional difficulty. It proposes simply to co-operate with any State by giving such State pecuniary aid"; and he thought that the resolution, as proposed by him, would be considered rather as the expression of a sentiment than as involving any constitutional question.

Mr. Hall, of Missouri, thought that if this proposition was adopted at all it should be by the votes of the free States, and come as a proposition from them to the slave States, affording them an inducement to put aside this subject of discord; that it ought not to be expected that members representing slaveholding constituencies should declare at once, and in advance of any proposition to them, for the emancipation of slavery.

The President said he saw and felt the force of the objection; it was a fearful responsibility, and every gentleman must do as he thought best; that he did not know how this scheme was received by the members from the free States; some of them had spoken to him and received it kindly; but for the most part they were as reserved and chary as we had been, and he could not tell how they would vote. And in reply to some expression of Mr. Hall as to his own opinion regarding slavery, he said he did not pretend to disguise his anti-slavery feeling; that he thought it was wrong, and should continue to think so; but that was not the question we had to deal with now. Slavery existed, and that, too, as well by the act of the North as of the South; and in any scheme to get rid of it the North as well as the South was morally bound to do its full and equal share. He thought the institution wrong and ought never to have existed; but yet he recognized the rights of property which had grown out of it, and would respect those rights as fully as similar rights in any other property; that property can exist and does legally exist. He thought such a law wrong, but the rights of property resulting must be respected; he would get rid of the odious law, not by violating the rights, but by encouraging the proposition and offering inducements to give it up.

Here the interview, so far as this subject is concerned, terminated by Mr. Crittenden's assuring the President that, whatever might be our final action, we all thought him solely moved by a high patriotism and sincere devotion to the happiness and glory of his country; and with that conviction we should consider respectfully the important suggestions he had made.

After some conversation on the current war news, we retired, and I immediately proceeded to my room and wrote out this paper. J. W. CRISFIELD.

We were present at the interview described in the foregoing paper of Mr. Crisfield, and we certify that the substance of what passed on the occasion is in this paper faithfully and fully given.

J. W. MENZIES, J. J. CRITTENDEN, R. MALLORY. March 10, 1862.

DRAWING CONCLUSIONS:

1. What does this document reveal about the competing political pressures Lincoln faced in early 1862 on the subject of slavery?
2. What does this document reveal about Lincoln's motivations for proposing gradual emancipation at the state level?

THE EMANCIPATION PROCLAMATION

Lincoln's pivotal shift in policy toward slavery came between March and July of 1862. In March of that year, he reassured representatives of the border slave states that he had no intention of interfering with the institution of slavery, regardless of the stance the border states took on his gradual emancipation proposal. In late July, however, he informed his cabinet of his intent to issue a proclamation of general emancipation in those areas in rebellion against the United States government. To understand how slavery came to an end in the Unites States, a detailed analysis of Lincoln's thought process during this pivotal four-month period is required.

6.1   ABRAHAM LINCOLN, "PROCLAMATION REVOKING GENERAL HUNTER'S ORDER OF MILITARY EMANCIPATION" (MAY 19, 1862)

In May 1862, a bold anti-slavery military order from one of Lincoln's generals forced the President to once again publicly address the issue of emancipation. General David Hunter, a man of strong anti-slavery views and an advocate of enlisting escaped slaves as soldiers, was the commander of Union forces operating along the South Carolina and Georgia coast. On May 9, 1862, Hunter issued a military order declaring all slaves in South Carolina, Georgia, and Florida to be forever free. (All but a few small coastal regions of the three states remained under Confederate control at the time of the order.) As he had with Frémont's proclamation the previous year, Lincoln quickly rescinded Hunter's order. The President also took the opportunity to publicly clarify his stance of the slavery issue. He reasserted his support for gradual emancipation and urged the border slave states to accept his proposal. While Lincoln's position on slavery remained constant, pay close attention to his changing tone.

GUIDING QUESTIONS:

1. What reasons does Lincoln cite for rescinding Hunter's emancipation order?
2. How does Lincoln try to persuade the border slave states to accept his gradual emancipation proposal?
3. How does the tone of Lincoln's message compare to earlier statements on the issue of slavery and emancipation?

PROCLAMATION REVOKING GENERAL HUNTER'S ORDER OF MILITARY EMANCIPATION OF MAY 9, 1862

MAY 19, 1862

By the President of The United States of America. A Proclamation.

Whereas there appears in the public prints, what purports to be a proclamation, of Major General Hunter, in the words and figures following, to wit:

Headquarters Department of the South,}

Hilton Head, S.C., May 9, 1862.}

General Orders No. 11.—The three States of Georgia, Florida and South Carolina, comprising the military department of the south, having deliberately declared themselves no longer under the protection of the United States of America, and having taken up arms against the said United States, it becomes a military necessity to declare them under martial law. This was accordingly done on the 25th day of April, 1862. Slavery and martial law in a free country are altogether incompatible; the persons in these three States—Georgia, Florida and South Carolina—heretofore held as slaves, are therefore declared forever free. DAVID HUNTER,

From Roy P. Basler, ed., *The Collected Works of Abraham Lincoln*, vol. 5 (New Brunswick, NJ: Rutgers University Press, 1953), 222–223.

(Official) Major General Commanding.

ED. W. SMITH, Acting Assistant Adjutant General.

And whereas the same is producing some excitement, and misunderstanding: therefore

I, Abraham Lincoln, president of the United States, proclaim and declare, that the government of the United States, had no knowledge, information, or belief, of an intention on the part of General Hunter to issue such a proclamation; nor has it yet, any authentic information that the document is genuine. And further, that neither General Hunter, nor any other commander, or person, has been authorized by the Government of the United States, to make proclamations declaring the slaves of any State free; and that the supposed proclamation, now in question, whether genuine or false, is altogether void, so far as respects such declaration.

I further make known that whether it be competent for me, as Commander-in-Chief of the Army and Navy, to declare the Slaves of any state or states, free, and whether at any time, in any case, it shall have become a necessity indispensable to the maintainance of the government, to exercise such supposed power, are questions which, under my responsibility, I reserve to myself, and which I can not feel justified in leaving to the decision of commanders in the field. These are totally different questions from those of police regulations in armies and camps.

On the sixth day of March last, by a special message, I recommended to Congress the adoption of a joint resolution to be substantially as follows:

Resolved, That the United States ought to co-operate with any State which may adopt a gradual abolishment of slavery, giving to such State pecuniary aid, to be used by such State in its discretion to compensate for the inconveniences, public and private, produced by such change of system.

The resolution, in the language above quoted, was adopted by large majorities in both branches of Congress, and now stands an authentic, definite, and solemn proposal of the nation to the States and people most immediately interested in the subject matter. To the people of those states I now earnestly appeal. I do not argue. I beseech you to make the arguments for yourselves. You can not if you would, be blind to the signs of the times. I beg of you a calm and enlarged consideration of them, ranging, if it may be, far above personal and partizan politics. This proposal makes common cause for a common object, casting no reproaches upon any. It acts not the pharisee. The change it contemplates would come gently as the dews of heaven, not rending or wrecking anything. Will you not embrace it? So much good has not been done, by one effort, in all past time, as, in the providence of God, it is now your high previlege to do. May the vast future not have to lament that you have neglected it.

In witness whereof, I have hereunto set my hand, and caused the seal of the United States to be affixed.

Done at the City of Washington this nineteenth day of May, in the year of our Lord one thousand eight hundred and sixty-two, and of the Independence of the United States the eighty-sixth. ABRAHAM LINCOLN.

DRAWING CONCLUSIONS:

1. What does Lincoln's response to Hunter's order reveal about the competing pressures Lincoln was subject to regarding the issue of slavery?
2. What does Lincoln's response suggest about his evolving thinking on the slavery issue?

6.2 GIDEON WELLES, EXCERPT FROM "THE HISTORY OF EMANCIPATION" (1872)

Gideon Welles was Lincoln's Secretary of the Navy. Several years after the war, Welles wrote this account of a conversation on July 13, 1862, among himself, Lincoln, and Secretary William H. Seward, in which Lincoln first shared his intention to issue a general proclamation of emancipation. Because it was written a decade after the conversation took place, some historians have questioned its reliability as evidence. Nonetheless, the document is among the most detailed accounts of the thought process that led Lincoln to issue the Emancipation Proclamation.

To understand Lincoln's decision, it must be placed in historical context. Between April and May of 1862, Union forces under the command of General George B. McClellan had gradually advanced on the Confederate capital of Richmond, Virginia, raising hopes that a military victory was at hand. For several weeks, McClellan remained stalled just outside the Confederate capital. Then, in late June, Confederate forces under General Robert E. Lee drove McClellan's forces back from Richmond. On July 8, Lincoln travelled to McClellan's camp in coastal Virginia to confer with the general and left the meeting with a clear understanding that the campaign had ended in failure. The spreading realization of McClellan's defeat prompted a wave of discouragement and pessimism throughout the North.

On July 12, Lincoln met once again with representatives from the border slave states to promote his gradual emancipation proposal but failed to make any significant progress. The next day, according to Gideon Welles, President Lincoln shared his decision in favor of a general proclamation of emancipation in the rebel states.

GUIDING QUESTIONS:

1. Why, according to Welles, was Lincoln so reluctant to issue a proclamation of general emancipation?
2. Why, according to Welles, did Lincoln ultimately decide to nonetheless issue a proclamation of general emancipation?

FROM "THE HISTORY OF EMANCIPATION"

GIDEON WELLES

On Sunday, the 13th of July, the day following this last hopeless interview, the President invited Mr. Seward and myself to accompany him in his carriage to the funeral of an infant child of Secretary Stanton. At that time Mr. Stanton occupied for a summer residence the house of a naval officer, some two or three miles west or northwest of Georgetown. It was on this occasion and this ride that he first mentioned to Mr. Seward and myself that he had about come to the conclusion that, if the rebels persisted in their war upon the Government, it would be a necessity and a duty on our part to liberate their slaves. He was convinced, he said, that we could not carry on a successful war by longer pursuing a temporizing and forbearing policy toward those who disregarded law and Constitution,

---

From Gideon Welles, "The History of Emancipation," *The Galaxy* 14 (December 1872), 842–843.

and were striving by every means to break up the Union. Decisive and extensive measures must be adopted. His reluctance to meddle with this question, around which there were thrown constitutional safeguards, and on which the whole Southern mind was sensitive, was great. He had tried various expedients to escape issuing an executive order emancipating the slaves, the last and only alternative, but it was forced upon him by the rebels themselves. He saw no escape. Turn which way he would, this disturbing element which caused the war rose up against us, and it was an insuperable obstacle to peace. He had entertained hopes that the border States, in view of what appeared to him inevitable if the war continued, would consent to some plan of prospective and compensated emancipation; but all his suggestions, some made as early as March, met with disfavor, although actual hostilities had then existed for a year. Congress was now about adjourning, and had done nothing final and conclusive—perhaps could do nothing on this question. He had since his return from the army the last week called the members of Congress from the border States together, and presented to them the difficulties which he encountered, in hopes they would be persuaded, in the gloomy condition of affairs, to take the initiative step toward emancipation; but they hesitated, and he apprehended would do nothing. Attached as most of them and a large majority of their constituents were to what they called their labor system, they felt it would be unjust for the Government which they supported to compel them to abandon that system, while the States in flagrant rebellion retained their slaves and were spared the sacrifice. A movement toward emancipation in the border States while slavery was recognized and permitted in the rebel States would, they believed, detach many from the Union cause and strengthen the insurrection. There was, he presumed, some foundation for their apprehension. What had been done and what he had heard satisfied him that a change of policy in the conduct of the war was necessary, and that emancipation of the slaves in the rebel States must precede that in the border States. The blow must fall first and foremost on them. Slavery was doomed. This war, brought upon the country by the slave-owners, would extinguish slavery, but the border States could not be induced to lead in that measure.

They would not consent to be convinced or persuaded to take the first step. Forced emancipation in the States which continued to resist the Government would of course be followed by voluntary emancipation in the loyal States, with the aid we might give them. Further efforts with the border States would, he thought, be useless. That was not the road to lead us out of this difficulty. We must take a different path. We wanted the army to strike more vigorous blows. The Administration must set an example, and strike at the heart of the rebellion. The country, he thought, was prepared for it. The army would be with us. War had removed constitutional obligations and restrictions with the declared rebel communities. The law required us to return the fugitives who escaped to us. This we could and must do with friends, but not with enemies. We invited all, bond and free, to desert those who were in flagrant war upon the Union and come to us; and uniting with us they must be made free from rebel authorities and rebel masters.

If there was no constitutional authority in the Government to emancipate the slaves, neither was there any authority, specified or reserved, for the slaveholders to resist the Government or secede from it. They could not at the same time throw off the Constitution and invoke its aid. Having made war upon the Government, they were subject to the incidents and calamities of war, and it was our duty to avail ourselves of every necessary measure to maintain the Union. If the rebels did not cease their war, they must take the consequences of war. He dwelt earnestly on the gravity, importance, and delicacy of the movement, which he had approached with reluctance, but he saw no evidence of a cessation of hostilities; said he had given the subject much thought, and had about come to the conclusion that it was a military necessity, absolutely essential to the preservation of the Union. We must free the slaves or be ourselves subdued. The slaves were undeniably an element of strength to those who had their service, and we must decide whether that element should be with us or against us. For a long time the subject had lain heavy on his mind. His interview with the representatives of the border States had forced him slowly but he believed correctly to this conclusion, and this present opportunity was the first occasion he had had of mentioning to any one his convictions of what in his opinion must be our course. He wished us to state frankly, not immediately, how the proposition of emancipation struck us, in case of the continued persistent resistance to Federal authority.

Mr. Seward remarked that the subject involved consequences so vast and momentous, legal and political, he should wish to bestow on it mature reflection before advising or giving a decisive answer; but his present opinion inclined to the measure as justifiable, and perhaps he might say expedient and necessary. These were essentially my views, more matured perhaps, for I had practically been dealing with slavery from the beginning as a wrecked institution. During that ride the subject was the absorbing theme, and before separating the President requested us to give it early, especial, and deliberate

consideration, for he was earnest in the conviction that the time had arrived when decisive action must be taken; that the Government could not be justified in any longer postponing it; that it was forced upon him as a necessity—it was thrust at him from various quarters; it occupied his mind and thoughts day and night. He repeated he had about come to a conclusion, driven home to him by the conference of the preceding day, but wished to know our views and hear any suggestions either of us might make.

DRAWING CONCLUSIONS:

1. What does Welles's account of his conversation with Lincoln and Seward reveal about the reasons that Lincoln ultimately embraced the abolition of slavery as a goal of the Union war effort?

6.3 SECOND CONFISCATION ACT (JULY 17, 1862)

As Lincoln embraced the idea of a general emancipation in the Confederate states, the Congress was also moving in a similar direction. In July 1862, the Congress passed the Second Confiscation Act, a piece of legislation that, while not as sweeping as the soon to be issued Emancipation Proclamation, went far beyond the previous year's First Confiscation Act on the issue of slavery.

GUIDING QUESTIONS:

1. The Second Confiscation Act declared several categories of slaves to be free. What categories of slaves, exactly, did the act declare to be free?
2. How did the provisions of the Second Confiscation Act regarding emancipation go beyond those of the First Confiscation Act?
3. What other policies regarding freed slaves and other individuals of African descent did the act put in place?

AN ACT TO SUPPRESS INSURRECTION, TO PUNISH TREASON AND REBELLION, TO SEIZE AND CONFISCATE THE PROPERTY OF REBELS, AND FOR OTHER PURPOSES.

Be it enacted by the Senate and House of Representatives of the United States of America in Congress assembled, That every person who shall hereafter commit the crime of treason against the United States, and shall be adjudged guilty thereof, shall suffer death, and all his slaves, if any, shall be declared and made free; or, at the discretion of the court, he shall be imprisoned for not less than five years and fined not less than ten thousand dollars, and all his slaves, if any, shall be declared and made free; said fine shall be levied and collected on any or all of the property, real and personal, excluding slaves, of which the said person so convicted was the owner at the time of committing the said crime, any sale or conveyance to the contrary notwithstanding.

Sec. 2. *And be it further enacted,* That if any person shall hereafter incite, set on foot, assist, or engage in any rebellion or insurrection against the authority of the United States, or the laws thereof, or shall give aid or comfort thereto, or shall engage in, or give aid and comfort to, any such existing rebellion or insurrection, and be convicted thereof, such person shall be punished by imprisonment for a period not exceeding ten years, or by a fine not exceeding ten thousand dollars, and by the liberation of all his slaves, if any he have; or by both of said punishments, at the discretion of the court.

Sec. 3. *And be it further enacted,* That every person guilty of either of the offences described in this act shall be forever incapable and disqualified to hold any office under the United States.

Sec. 4. *And be it further enacted,* That this act shall not be construed in any way to affect or alter the prosecution, conviction, or punishment of any person or persons guilty of treason against the United States before the passage of this act, unless such person is convicted under this act.

Sec. 5. *And be it further enacted,* That, to insure the speedy termination of the present rebellion, it shall be the duty of the President of the United States to cause the seizure of all the estate and property, money, stocks, credits, and effects of the persons hereinafter named in this section, and to apply and

From *The Statutes at Large, Treaties, and Proclamations of the United States of America,* 37th Congress, 2nd Session, 589–592.

use the same and the proceeds thereof for the support of the army of the United States, that is to say:

First. Of any person hereafter acting as an officer of the army or navy of the rebels in arms against the government of the United States.

Secondly. Of any person hereafter acting as President, Vice-President, member of Congress, judge of any court, cabinet officer, foreign minister, commissioner or consul of the so-called confederate states of America.

Thirdly. Of any person acting as governor of a state, member of a convention or legislature, or judge of any court of any of the so-called confederate states of America.

Fourthly. Of any person who, having held an office of honor, trust, or profit in the United States, shall hereafter hold an office in the so-called confederate states of America.

Fifthly. Of any person hereafter holding any office or agency under the government of the so-called confederate states of America, or under any of the several states of the said confederacy, or the laws thereof, whether such office or agency be national, state, or municipal in its name or character: *Provided*, That the persons, thirdly, fourthly, and fifthly above described shall have accepted their appointment or election since the date of the pretended ordinance of secession of the state, or shall have taken an oath of allegiance to, or to support the constitution of the so-called confederate states.

Sixthly. Of any person who, owning property in any loyal State or Territory of the United States, or in the District of Columbia, shall hereafter assist and give aid and comfort to such rebellion; and all sales, transfers, or conveyances of any such property shall be null and void; and it shall be a sufficient bar to any suit brought by such person for the possession or the use of such property, or any of it, to allege and prove that he is one of the persons described in this section.

SEC. 6. *And be it further enacted*, That if any person within any State or Territory of the United States, other than those named as aforesaid, after the passage of this act, being engaged in armed rebellion against the government of the United States, or aiding or abetting such rebellion, shall not, within sixty days after public warning and proclamation duly given and made by the President of the United States, cease to aid, countenance, and abet such rebellion, and return to his allegiance to the United States, all the estate and property, moneys, stocks, and credits of such person shall be liable to seizure as aforesaid, and it shall be the duty of the President to seize and use them as aforesaid or the proceeds thereof. And all sales, transfers, or conveyances, of any such property after the expiration of the said sixty days from the date of such warning and proclamation shall be null and void; and it shall be a sufficient bar to any suit brought by such person for the possession or the use of such property, or any of it, to allege and prove that he is one of the persons described in this section.

SEC. 7. *And be it further enacted*, That to secure the condemnation and sale of any of such property, after the same shall have been seized, so that it may be made available for the purpose aforesaid, proceedings in rem shall be instituted in the name of the United States in any district court thereof, or in any territorial court, or in the United States district court for the District of Columbia, within which the property above described, or any part thereof, may be found, or into which the same, if movable, may first be brought, which proceedings shall conform as nearly as may be to proceedings in admiralty or revenue cases, and if said property, whether real or personal, shall be found to have belonged to a person engaged in rebellion, or who has given aid or comfort thereto, the same shall be condemned as enemies' property and become the property of the United States, and may be disposed of as the court shall decree and the proceeds thereof paid into the treasury of the United States for the purposes aforesaid.

SEC. 8. *And be it further enacted*, That the several courts aforesaid shall have power to make such orders, establish such forms of decree and sale, and direct such deeds and conveyances to be executed and delivered by the marshals thereof where real estate shall be the subject of sale, as shall fitly and efficiently effect the purposes of this act, and vest in the purchasers of such property good and valid titles thereto. And the said courts shall have power to allow such fees and charges of their officers as shall be reasonable and proper in the premises.

SEC. 9. *And be it further enacted*, That all slaves of persons who shall hereafter be engaged in rebellion against the government of the United States, or who shall in any way give aid or comfort thereto, escaping from such persons and taking refuge within the lines of the army; and all slaves captured from such persons or deserted by them and coming under the control of the government of the United States; and all slaves of such person found on [or] being within any place occupied by rebel forces and afterwards occupied by the forces of the United States, shall be deemed captives of war, and shall be forever free of their servitude, and not again held as slaves.

SEC. 10. *And be it further enacted*, That no slave escaping into any State, Territory, or the District of Columbia, from any other State, shall be delivered up, or in any way impeded or hindered of his liberty, except for crime, or some offence against the laws, unless the person claiming said fugitive shall first make oath that the person to whom the labor or service of such fugitive is alleged to be due is his lawful owner, and has not borne arms against the United States in the present rebellion, nor in any way given aid and comfort thereto; and no person engaged in the military or naval service of the United States shall, under any pretence whatever, assume to decide on the validity of the claim of any person to the service or labor of any other person, or surrender up any such person to the claimant, on pain of being dismissed from the service.

SEC. 11. *And be it further enacted*, That the President of the United States is authorized to employ as many persons of African descent as he may deem necessary and proper for the suppression of this rebellion, and for this purpose he may organize and use them in such manner as he may judge best for the public welfare.

SEC. 12. *And be it further enacted*, That the President of the United States is hereby authorized to make provision for the transportation, colonization, and settlement, in some tropical country beyond the limits of the United States, of such persons of the African race, made free by the provisions of this act, as may be willing to emigrate, having first obtained the consent of the government of said country to their protection and settlement within the same, with all the rights and privileges of freemen.

SEC. 13. *And be it further enacted*, That the President is hereby authorized, at any time hereafter, by proclamation, to extend to persons who may have participated in the existing rebellion in any State or part thereof, pardon and amnesty, with such exceptions and at such time and on such conditions as he may deem expedient for the public welfare.

SEC. 14. *And be it further enacted*, That the courts of the United States shall have full power to institute proceedings, make orders and decrees, issue process, and do all other things necessary to carry this act into effect.

APPROVED, July 17, 1862.

DRAWING CONCLUSIONS:

1. What can we learn about the evolution of congressional policy toward slavery from the Second Confiscation Act?

2. What does this piece of legislation reveal about the impact of runaway slaves on federal policymakers?

3. Why do you think that the law included the provision in section 12 for the possible colonization of freed people to a tropical region outside of the United States?

6.4   ABRAHAM LINCOLN TO HORACE GREELEY (AUGUST 22, 1862)

In August 1862, influential newspaper editor Horace Greeley published an open letter to President Lincoln urging him to more aggressively implement to the provisions of the Second Confiscation Act. Greeley, of course, did not know that Lincoln had already decided to issue an emancipation proclamation declaring all slaves within rebel controlled areas to be forever free. Lincoln's response to Greeley (which Lincoln could correctly assume Greeley would print in his newspaper) is among his most quoted statements on the subject of slavery, particularly by those who consider it evidence of Lincoln's lack of commitment to emancipation. When analyzing Lincoln's letter to Greeley, it is important to remember that Lincoln had already decided to issue the Emancipation Proclamation.

GUIDING QUESTIONS:

1.   What does Lincoln tell Greeley will determine his stance on the issue of emancipation?
2.   Keeping in mind that Lincoln had already decided to issue a proclamation declaring those enslaved in rebel areas to be forever free, what might be Lincoln's motive in writing this letter to Greeley?

LINCOLN TO HORACE GREELEY

HON. HORACE GREELY: EXECUTIVE MANSION, WASHINGTON, AUGUST 22, 1862.

Dear Sir

I have just read yours of the 19th. addressed to myself through the New-York Tribune. If there be in it any statements, or assumptions of fact, which I may know to be erroneous, I do not, now and here, controvert them. If there be in it any inferences which I may believe to be falsely drawn, I do not now and here, argue against them. If there be perceptable in it an impatient and dictatorial tone, I waive it in deference to an old friend, whose heart I have always supposed to be right.

As to the policy I "seem to be pursuing" as you say, I have not meant to leave any one in doubt.

I would save the Union. I would save it the shortest way under the Constitution. The sooner the national authority can be restored; the nearer the Union will be "the Union as it was." If there be those who would not save the Union, unless they could at the same time save slavery, I do not agree with them. If there be those who would not save the Union unless they could at the same time destroy slavery, I do not agree with them. My paramount object in this struggle is to save the Union, and is not either to save or to destroy slavery. If I could save the Union without freeing any slave I would do it, and if I could save it by freeing all the slaves I would do it; and if I could save it by freeing some and leaving others alone I would also do that. What I do about slavery, and the colored race, I do because I believe it helps to save the Union; and what I forbear, I forbear because I do not believe it would help to save the Union. I shall do less whenever I shall believe what I am doing hurts the cause, and I shall do

From Roy P. Basler, ed., *The Collected Works of Abraham Lincoln*, vol. 5 (New Brunswick, NJ: Rutgers University Press, 1953), 388–389.

more whenever I shall believe doing more will help the cause. I shall try to correct errors when shown to be errors; and I shall adopt new views so fast as they shall appear to be true views.

I have here stated my purpose according to my view of official duty; and I intend no modification of my oft-expressed personal wish that all men every where could be free. Yours,

A. LINCOLN

DRAWING CONCLUSIONS:

1. Does this document tell us more about Lincoln's personal political motives or more about his political strategy for "selling" the idea of emancipation? Why? What can we learn from this document regarding his strategy to sell the Emancipation Proclamation?

6.5 PRELIMINARY AND FINAL EMANCIPATION PROCLAMATIONS (SEPTEMBER 22, 1862, AND JANUARY 1, 1863)

Acting in his military capacity as Commander-in-Chief, Lincoln issued his Preliminary Emancipation on September 22, 1862. The preliminary proclamation announced Lincoln's intention, as of January 1 of the following year, to declare all persons held as slaves in areas in rebellion against the United States to be forever free. As promised, Lincoln issued his final Emancipation Proclamation on January 1, 1863. There are subtle differences between the two documents that can serve as clues regarding Lincoln's evolving stance on issues of slavery and race.

GUIDING QUESTIONS:

1. Besides the promised emancipation of slaves in the rebel areas, what other policies regarding slavery and race were included in the Preliminary Emancipation Proclamation?
2. Besides declaring those held as slaves in rebel areas to be free, what other policies regarding slavery and race were included in the Final Emancipation Proclamation?
3. What differences are there between the policies contained in the Preliminary and Final Emancipation Proclamations?

PRELIMINARY EMANCIPATION PROCLAMATION

SEPTEMBER 22, 1862

By the President of the
United States of America
A Proclamation.

I, Abraham Lincoln, President of the United States of America, and Commander-in-chief of the Army and Navy thereof, do hereby proclaim and declare that hereafter, as heretofore, the war will be prosecuted for the object of practically restoring the constitutional relation between the United States, and each of the states, and the people thereof, in which states that relation is, or may be suspended, or disturbed.

That it is my purpose, upon the next meeting of Congress to again recommend the adoption of a practical measure tendering pecuniary aid to the free acceptance or rejection of all slave-states, so called, the people whereof may not then be in rebellion against the United States, and which states, may then have voluntarily adopted, or thereafter may voluntarily adopt, immediate, or gradual abolishment of slavery within their respective limits; and that the effort to colonize persons of African descent, with their consent, upon this continent, or elsewhere, with the previously obtained consent of the Governments existing there, will be continued.

That on the first day of January in the year of our Lord, one thousand eight hundred and sixty-three, all persons held as slaves within any state, or designated part of a state, the people whereof shall then be in rebellion against the United States shall be then, thenceforward, and forever free; and the executive government of the United States, including the military and naval authority thereof, will recognize and

From Roy P. Basler, ed., *The Collected Works of Abraham Lincoln*, vol. 5 (New Brunswick, NJ: Rutgers University Press, 1953), 433–436.

maintain the freedom of such persons, and will do no act or acts to repress such persons, or any of them, in any efforts they may make for their actual freedom.

That the executive will, on the first day of January aforesaid, by proclamation, designate the States, and parts of states, if any, in which the people thereof respectively, shall then be in rebellion against the United States; and the fact that any state, or the people thereof shall, on that day be, in good faith represented in the Congress of the United States, by members chosen thereto, at elections wherein a majority of the qualified voters of such state shall have participated, shall, in the absence of strong countervailing testimony, be deemed conclusive evidence that such state and the people thereof, are not then in rebellion against the United States.

That attention is hereby called to an act of Congress entitled "An act to make an additional Article of War" approved March 13, 1862, and which act is in the words and figure following: Be it enacted by the Senate and House of Representatives of the United States of America in Congress assembled, That hereafter the following shall be promulgated as an additional article of war for the government of the army of the United States, and shall be obeyed and observed as such:

Article—All officers or persons in the military or naval service of the United States are prohibited from employing any of the forces under their respective commands for the purpose of returning fugitives from service or labor, who may have escaped from any persons to whom such service or labor is claimed to be due, and any officer who shall be found guilty by a court-martial of violating this article shall be dismissed from the service.

SEC. 2. And be it further enacted, That this act shall take effect from and after its passage.

Also to the ninth and tenth sections of an act entitled "An Act to suppress Insurrection, to punish Treason and Rebellion, to seize and confiscate property of rebels, and for other purposes," approved July 17, 1862, and which sections are in the words and figures following:

SEC. 9. And be it further enacted, That all slaves of persons who shall hereafter be engaged in rebellion against the government of the United States, or who shall in any way give aid or comfort thereto, escaping from such persons and taking refuge within the lines of the army; and all slaves captured from such persons or deserted by them and coming under the control of the government of the United States; and all slaves of such persons found on (or) being within any place occupied by rebel forces and afterwards occupied by the forces of the United States, shall be deemed captives of war, and shall be forever free of their servitude and not again held as slaves.

SEC. 10. And be it further enacted, That no slave escaping into any State, Territory, or the District of Columbia, from any other State, shall be delivered up, or in any way impeded or hindered of his liberty, except for crime, or some offence against the laws, unless the person claiming said fugitive shall first make oath that the person to whom the labor or service of such fugitive is alleged to be due is his lawful owner, and has not borne arms against the United States in the present rebellion, nor in any way given aid and comfort thereto; and no person engaged in the military or naval service of the United States shall, under any pretence whatever, assume to decide on the validity of the claim of any person to the service or labor of any other person, or surrender up any such person to the claimant, on pain of being dismissed from the service.

And I do hereby enjoin upon and order all persons engaged in the military and naval service of the United States to observe, obey, and enforce, within their respective spheres of service, the act, and sections above recited.

And the executive will in due time recommend that all citizens of the United States who shall have remained loyal thereto throughout the rebellion, shall (upon the restoration of the constitutional relation between the United States, and their respective states, and people, if that relation shall have been suspended or disturbed) be compensated for all losses by acts of the United States, including the loss of slaves.

In witness whereof, I have hereunto set my hand, and caused the seal of the United States to be affixed.

Done at the City of Washington, this twenty second day of September, in the year of our Lord, one thousand eight hundred and sixty two, and of the Independence of the United States, the eighty seventh.

By the President: ABRAHAM LINCOLN

EMANCIPATION PROCLAMATION

JANUARY 1, 1863

By the President of the United States of America: A Proclamation.

Whereas, on the twenty second day of September, in the year of our Lord one thousand eight hundred and sixty two, a proclamation was issued by the President of the United States, containing, among other things, the following, to wit:

"That on the first day of January, in the year of our Lord one thousand eight hundred and sixty-three, all persons held as slaves within any State or designated part of a State, the people whereof shall then be in rebellion against the United States, shall be then, thenceforward, and forever free; and the Executive Government of the United States, including the military and naval authority thereof, will recognize and maintain the freedom of such persons, and will do no act or acts to repress such persons, or any of them, in any efforts they may make for their actual freedom.

"That the Executive will, on the first day of January aforesaid, by proclamation, designate the States and parts of States, if any, in which the people thereof, respectively, shall then be in rebellion against the United States; and the fact that any State, or the people thereof, shall on that day be, in good faith, represented in the Congress of the United States by members chosen thereto at elections wherein a majority of the qualified voters of such State shall have participated, shall, in the absence of strong countervailing testimony, be deemed conclusive evidence that such State, and the people thereof, are not then in rebellion against the United States."

Now, therefore I, Abraham Lincoln, President of the United States, by virtue of the power in me vested as Commander-in-Chief, of the Army and Navy of the United States in time of actual armed rebellion against authority and government of the United States, and as a fit and necessary war measure for suppressing said rebellion, do, on this first day of January, in the year of our Lord one thousand eight hundred and sixty three, and in accordance with my purpose so to do publicly proclaimed for the full period of one hundred days, from the day first above mentioned, order and designate as the States and parts of States wherein the people thereof respectively, are this day in rebellion against the United States, the following, to wit:

Arkansas, Texas, Louisiana, (except the Parishes of St. Bernard, Plaquemines, Jefferson, St. Johns, St. Charles, St. James[,] Ascension, Assumption, Terrebonne, Lafourche, St. Mary, St. Martin, and Orleans, including the City of New-Orleans) Mississippi, Alabama, Florida, Georgia, South-Carolina, North-Carolina, and Virginia, (except the forty-eight counties designated as West Virginia, and also the counties of Berkley, Accomac, Northampton, Elizabeth-City, York, Princess Ann, and Norfolk, including the cities of Norfolk & Portsmouth [)]; and which excepted parts are, for the present, left precisely as if this proclamation were not issued.

And by virtue of the power, and for the purpose aforesaid, I do order and declare that all persons held as slaves within said designated States, and parts of States, are, and henceforward shall be free; and that the Executive government of the United States, including the military and naval authorities thereof, will recognize and maintain the freedom of said persons.

And I hereby enjoin upon the people so declared to be free to abstain from all violence, unless in necessary self-defence; and I recommend to them that, in all cases when allowed, they labor faithfully for reasonable wages.

And I further declare and make known, that such persons of suitable condition, will be received into

---

From Roy P. Basler, ed., *The Collected Works of Abraham Lincoln*, vol. 6 (New Brunswick, NJ: Rutgers University Press, 1953), 28–30.

the armed service of the United States to garrison forts, positions, stations, and other places, and to man vessels of all sorts in said service.

And upon this act, sincerely believed to be an act of justice, warranted by the Constitution, upon military necessity, I invoke the considerate judgment of mankind, and the gracious favor of Almighty God.

In witness whereof, I have hereunto set my hand and caused the seal of the United States to be affixed.

Done at the City of Washington, this first day of January, in the year of our Lord one thousand eight

hundred and sixty three, and of the Independence of the United States of America the eighty-seventh.

By the President: ABRAHAM LINCOLN

DRAWING CONCLUSIONS:

1. What do the differences between the Preliminary and Final Emancipation Proclamations indicate about Lincoln's evolving thinking on issues of slavery and race and their role in his wartime strategy?

6.6 FREDERICK DOUGLASS, "MEN OF COLOR, TO ARMS!" (MARCH 1863)

Following the Emancipation Proclamation, the Union Army began to aggressively recruit black soldiers, both among escaped and freed slaves and among the free black population of the North. Famed black abolitionist Frederick Douglass was among the most energetic advocates of African American enlistment. In this article, published shortly after the final Emancipation Proclamation was issued, Douglass argues that black men have an obligation to join the Union struggle. Although this document does not provide direct evidence regarding Lincoln's motives for making emancipation a war aim, it provides a sense of the impact of that decision on the conduct of the war. During the Civil War, 179,000 black men (mostly former slaves) enlisted in the Union Army; and by the time of the Confederate surrender, black soldiers comprised about 15% of Union forces. In addition, about 20,000 African American sailors served in the Union Navy.

GUIDING QUESTIONS:

1. What reasons does Douglass give for black men to join the Union Army?
2. What impact did the Emancipation Proclamation have on Douglass?

MEN OF COLOR, TO ARMS!

FREDERICK DOUGLASS

When first the rebel cannon shattered the walls of Sumter and drove away its starving garrison, I predicted that the war then and there inaugurated would not be fought out entirely by white men. Every month's experience during these dreary years has confirmed that opinion. A war undertaken and brazenly carried on for the perpetual enslavement of colored men, calls logically and loudly for colored men to help suppress it. Only a moderate share of sagacity was needed to see that the arm of the slave was the best defense against the arm of the slaveholder. Hence with every reverse to the national arms, with every exulting shout of victory raised by the slaveholding rebels, I have implored the imperiled nation to unchain against her foes, her powerful black hand.

Slowly and reluctantly that appeal is beginning to be heeded. Stop not now to complain that it was not heeded sooner. It may or it may not have been best that it should not. This is not the time to discuss that question. Leave it to the future. When the war is over, the country is saved, peace is established, and the black man's rights are secured, as they will be, history with an impartial hand will dispose of that and sundry other questions. Action! Action! not criticism, is the plain duty of this hour. Words are now useful only as they stimulate to blows. The office of speech now is only to point out when, where, and how to strike to the best advantage.

There is no time to delay. The tide is at its flood that leads on to fortune. From East to West, from North to South, the sky is written all over, "Now or never." Liberty won by white men would lose half its luster. "Who would be free themselves must strike the blow." "Better even die free, than to live slaves." This is the sentiment of every brave colored man amongst us.

There are weak and cowardly men in all nations. We have them amongst us. They tell you this is the

From *Douglass' Monthly*, March 1863.

"white man's war"; and you will be "no better off after than before the war"; that the getting of you into the army is to "sacrifice you on the first opportunity." Believe them not; cowards themselves, they do not wish to have their cowardice shamed by your brave example. Leave them to their timidity, or to whatever motive may hold them back.

I have not thought lightly of the words I am now addressing you. The counsel I give comes of close observation of the great struggle now in progress, and of the deep conviction that this is your hour and mine. In good earnest then, and after the best deliberation, I now for the first time during this war feel at liberty to call and counsel you to arms.

By every consideration which binds you to your enslaved fellow countrymen, and the peace and welfare of your country; by every aspiration which you cherish for the freedom and equality of yourselves and your children; by all the ties of blood and identity which make us one with the brave black men now fighting our battles in Louisiana and in South Carolina, I urge you to fly to arms, and smite with death the power that would bury the government and your liberty in the same hopeless grave.

I wish I could tell you that the State of New York calls you to this high honor. For the moment her constituted authorities are silent on the subject. They will speak by and by, and doubtless on the right side; but we are not compelled to wait for her. We can get at the throat of treason and slavery through the State of Massachusetts. She was the first in the War of Independence; first to break the chains of her slaves; first to make the black man equal before the law; first to admit colored children to her common schools, and she was first to answer with her blood the alarm cry of the nation, when its capital was menaced by rebels. You know her patriotic governor, and you know Charles Sumner. I need not add more.

Massachusetts now welcomes you to arms as soldiers. She has but a small colored population from which to recruit. She has full leave of the general government to send one regiment to the war, and she has undertaken to do it. Go quickly and help fill up the first colored regiment from the North. I am authorized to assure you that you will receive the same wages, the same rations, the same equipments, the same protection, the same treatment, and the same bounty, secured to the white soldiers. You will be led by able and skillful officers, men who will take especial pride in your efficiency and success. They will be quick to accord to you all the honor you shall merit by your valor, and see that your rights and feelings are respected by other soldiers. I have assured myself on these points, and can speak with authority.

More than twenty years of unswerving devotion to our common cause may give me some humble claim to be trusted at this momentous crisis. I will not argue. To do so implies hesitation and doubt, and you do not hesitate. You do not doubt. The day dawns; the morning star is bright upon the horizon! The iron gate of our prison stands half open. One gallant rush from the North will fling it wide open, while four millions of our brothers and sisters shall march out into liberty. The chance is now given you to end in a day the bondage of centuries, and to rise in one bound from social degradation to the place of common equality with all other varieties of men.

Remember Denmark Vesey of Charleston; remember Nathaniel Turner of Southampton; remember Shields Green and Copeland, who followed noble John Brown, and fell as glorious martyrs for the cause of the slave. Remember that in a contest with oppression, the Almighty has no attribute which can take sides with oppressors.

The case is before you. This is our golden opportunity. Let us accept it, and forever wipe out the dark reproaches unsparingly hurled against us by our enemies. Let us win for ourselves the gratitude of our country, and the best blessings of our posterity through all time. The nucleus of this first regiment is now in camp at Readville, a short distance from Boston. I will undertake to forward to Boston all persons adjudged fit to be mustered into the regiment, who shall apply to me at any time within the next two weeks.

DRAWING CONCLUSIONS:

1. What does Douglass' reaction to the Emancipation Proclamation suggest about the proclamation's impact?

6.7   ABRAHAM LINCOLN TO SALMON P. CHASE
(SEPTEMBER 2, 1863)

Secretary of the Treasury Salmon P. Chase was the member of Lincoln's cabinet with the closest ties with the abolitionist movement. In the months following the issuing of the final Emancipation Proclamation, abolitionists lobbied Lincoln to expand its reach beyond those areas in active rebellion against the government. In this letter to Chase, Lincoln explains his reasons for restricting the proclamation's reach.

GUIDING QUESTIONS:

1. Why does Lincoln say that he cannot expand the reach of the Emancipation Proclamation beyond those areas actively in rebellion against the government?

LINCOLN TO SALMON P. CHASE

HON. S. P. CHASE. EXECUTIVE MANSION, WASHINGTON, SEPTEMBER 2. 1863.

My dear Sir:

Knowing your great anxiety that the emancipation proclamation shall now be applied to certain parts of Virginia and Louisiana which were exempted from it last January, I state briefly what appear to me to be difficulties in the way of such a step. The original proclamation has no constitutional or legal justification, except as a military measure. The exemptions were made because the military necessity did not apply to the exempted localities. Nor does that necessity apply to them now any more than it did then. If I take the step must I not do so, without the argument of military necessity, and so, without any argument, except the one that I think the measure politically expedient, and morally right? Would I not thus give up all footing upon constitution or law? Would I not thus be in the boundless field of absolutism? Could this pass unnoticed, or unresisted? Could it fail to be perceived that without any further stretch, I might do the same in Delaware, Maryland, Kentucky, Tennessee, and Missouri; and even change any law in any state? Would not many of our own friends shrink away appalled? Would it not lose us the elections, and with them, the very cause we seek to advance?

DRAWING CONCLUSIONS:

1. What can we learn from this letter about the reasons that Lincoln limited the Emancipation Proclamation to those areas deemed in rebellion against the United States?

From Roy P. Basler, ed., *The Collected Works of Abraham Lincoln*, vol. 6 (New Brunswick, NJ: Rutgers University Press, 1953), 428–429.

6.8 ABRAHAM LINCOLN TO ALBERT G. HODGES (APRIL 4, 1864)

In April 1865, Governor Thomas Bramlette and Senator Archibald Dixon of Kentucky, along with Kentucky newspaper editor Albert G. Hodges, met with President Lincoln to discuss concerns they had with the black military enlistment policy in the state. After the meeting, Hodges asked Lincoln for a copy of remarks the President had made on the topic of emancipation. Lincoln responded to Hodges in a letter in which the President provides a summary of the thought process that he says led him to issue the Emancipation Proclamation.

GUIDING QUESTIONS:

1. What does Lincoln tell Hodges was the reason for the timing of the Emancipation Proclamation?
2. What does Lincoln say was his reason for issuing the Emancipation Proclamation?
3. How, according to Lincoln, did the Emancipation Proclamation benefit the Union war effort?

LINCOLN TO ALBERT G. HODGES

A. G. HODGES, ESQ EXECUTIVE MANSION,

FRANKFORT, KY. WASHINGTON, APRIL 4, 1864.

My dear Sir: You ask me to put in writing the substance of what I verbally said the other day, in your presence, to Governor Bramlette and Senator Dixon. It was about as follows:

"I am naturally anti-slavery. If slavery is not wrong, nothing is wrong. I can not remember when I did not so think, and feel. And yet I have never understood that the Presidency conferred upon me an unrestricted right to act officially upon this judgment and feeling. It was in the oath I took that I would, to the best of my ability, preserve, protect, and defend the Constitution of the United States. I could not take the office without taking the oath. Nor was it my view that I might take an oath to get power, and break the oath in using the power. I understood, too, that in ordinary civil administration this oath even forbade me to practically indulge my primary abstract judgment on the moral question of slavery. I had publicly declared this many times, and in many ways. And I aver that, to this day, I have done no official act in mere deference to my abstract judgment and feeling on slavery. I did understand however, that my oath to preserve the constitution to the best of my ability, imposed upon me the duty of preserving, by every indispensable means, that government—that nation—of which that constitution was the organic law. Was it possible to lose the nation, and yet preserve the constitution? By general law life and limb must be protected; yet often a limb must be amputated to save a life; but a life is never wisely given to save a limb. I felt that measures, otherwise unconstitutional, might become lawful, by becoming indispensable to the preservation of the constitution, through the preservation of the nation. Right or wrong, I assumed this ground, and now avow it. I could not feel that, to the best of my ability, I had even tried to preserve the constitution, if, to save slavery, or any minor matter, I should permit the wreck of government, country, and Constitution

From Roy P. Basler, ed., *The Collected Works of Abraham Lincoln*, vol. 7 (New Brunswick, NJ: Rutgers University Press, 1953), 281–283.

all together. When, early in the war, Gen. Fremont attempted military emancipation, I forbade it, because I did not then think it an indispensable necessity. When a little later, Gen. Cameron, then Secretary of War, suggested the arming of the blacks, I objected, because I did not yet think it an indispensable necessity. When, still later, Gen. Hunter attempted military emancipation, I again forbade it, because I did not yet think the indispensable necessity had come. When, in March, and May, and July 1862 I made earnest, and successive appeals to the border states to favor compensated emancipation, I believed the indispensable necessity for military emancipation, and arming the blacks would come, unless averted by that measure. They declined the proposition; and I was, in my best judgment, driven to the alternative of either surrendering the Union, and with it, the Constitution, or of laying strong hand upon the colored element. I chose the latter. In choosing it, I hoped for greater gain than loss; but of this, I was not entirely confident. More than a year of trial now shows no loss by it in our foreign relations, none in our home popular sentiment, none in our white military force,—no loss by it any how or anywhere. On the contrary, it shows a gain of quite a hundred and thirty thousand soldiers, seamen, and laborers. These are palpable facts, about which, as facts, there can be no cavilling. We have the men; and we could not have had them without the measure.

["]And now let any Union man who complains of the measure, test himself by writing down in one line that he is for subduing the rebellion by force of arms; and in the next, that he is for taking these hundred and thirty thousand men from the Union side, and placing them where they would be but for the measure he condemns. If he can not face his case so stated, it is only because he can not face the truth.["]

I add a word which was not in the verbal conversation. In telling this tale I attempt no compliment to my own sagacity. I claim not to have controlled events, but confess plainly that events have controlled me. Now, at the end of three years struggle the nation's condition is not what either party, or any man devised, or expected. God alone can claim it. Whither it is tending seems plain. If God now wills the removal of a great wrong, and wills also that we of the North as well as you of the South, shall pay fairly for our complicity in that wrong, impartial history will find therein new cause to attest and revere the justice and goodness of God. Yours truly

A. LINCOLN

DRAWING CONCLUSIONS:

1. What does this letter suggest about the reasons that Lincoln embraced emancipation as a Union war aim?

6.9 F.B. CARPENTER, EXCERPT FROM *SIX MONTHS IN THE WHITE HOUSE* (1866)

Francis B. Carpenter was a well-known painter who gained prominence producing portraits of notable public figures, including Presidents Millard Fillmore, Franklin Pierce, and John Tyler. In February 1864, Lincoln granted Carpenter permission to produce a painting that would commemorate the Emancipation Proclamation. Carpenter spent the next several months completing work on the painting that he entitled *First Reading of the Emancipation Proclamation of President Lincoln.* (The painting was later donated to the US Congress and today hangs in the Capitol.) Carpenter happened to be with the President in the White House during a meeting between Lincoln and a delegation of visiting abolitionists. In a memoir he published in 1866, Carpenter included an account of this meeting at which Lincoln explained the timing of the Emancipation Proclamation.

FIGURE 1. FRANCIS B. CARPENTER, FIRST READING OF THE EMANCIPATION PROCLAMATION OF PRESIDENT LINCOLN (1864).
Source: Painted by F.B. Carpenter; engraved by A.H. Ritchie. Library of Congress Prints and Photographs Division Washington, D.C. 20540 USA

GUIDING QUESTIONS:

1. According to Carpenter, what reasons did Lincoln provide for the timing of the Emancipation Proclamation?
2. According to Carpenter, what did Lincoln tell the visiting abolitionists was his motive for issuing the Emancipation Proclamation?

FROM SIX MONTHS AT THE WHITE HOUSE WITH ABRAHAM LINCOLN

F.B. CARPENTER

Mr. George Thompson, the English anti-slavery orator, delivered an address in the House of Representatives, to a large audience, April 6th, 1864. Among the distinguished persons present was President Lincoln, who was greatly interested. The following morning, Mr. Thompson and party, consisting of Rev. John Pierpont, Oliver Johnson, formerly President of the Anti-Slavery Society of New York, and the Hon. Lewis Clephane, of Washington, called at the White House. The President was alone when their names were announced, with the exception of myself. Dropping all business, he ordered the party to be immediately admitted. Greeting them very cordially, the gentlemen took seats, and Mr. Thompson commenced conversation by referring to the condition of public sentiment in England in regard to the great conflict the nation was passing through. He said the aristocracy and the "money interest" were desirous of seeing the Union broken up, but that the great heart of the masses beat in sympathy with the North. They instinctively felt that the cause of liberty was bound up with our success in putting down the Rebellion, and the struggle was being watched with the deepest anxiety.

Mr. Lincoln thereupon said: "Mr. Thompson, the people of Great Britain, and of other foreign governments, were in one great error in reference to this conflict. They seemed to think that, the moment I was President, I had the power to abolish slavery, forgetting that, before I could have any power whatever, I had to take the oath to support the Constitution of the United States, and execute the laws as I found them. When the Rebellion broke out, my duty did not admit of a question. That was, first, by all strictly lawful means to endeavor to maintain the integrity of the government. I did not consider that I had a *right* to touch the 'State' institution of 'Slavery' until all other measures for restoring the Union had failed. The paramount idea of the constitution is the preservation of the Union. It may not be specified in so many words, but that this was the idea of its founders is evident; for, without the Union, the constitution would be worthless. It seems clear, then, that in the last extremity, if any local institution threatened the existence of the Union, the Executive could not hesitate as to his duty. In our case, the moment came when I felt that slavery must die that the nation might live! I have sometimes used the illustration in this connection of a man with a diseased limb, and his surgeon. So long as there is a chance of the patient's restoration, the surgeon is solemnly bound to try to save both life *and* limb; but when the crisis comes, and the limb must be sacrificed as the only chance of saving the life, no honest man will hesitate.

"Many of my strongest supporters urged *Emancipation* before I thought it indispensable, and, I may say, before I thought the country ready for it. It is my conviction that, had the proclamation been issued even six months earlier than it was, public sentiment would not have sustained it. Just so, as to the subsequent action in reference to enlisting blacks in the Border States. The step, taken sooner, could not, in my judgment, have been carried out. A man watches his pear-tree day after day, impatient for the ripening of the fruit. Let him attempt to *force* the process, and he may spoil both fruit and tree. But let him patiently *wait*, and the ripe pear at length falls into his lap! We have seen this great revolution in public sentiment slowly but *surely* progressing, so that, when final action came, the opposition was not strong enough to defeat the purpose. I can now solemnly assert," he concluded, "that I have a clear conscience in regard to my action on this momentous question. I have done what no man could have helped doing, standing in my place."

DRAWING CONCLUSIONS:

1. What does this document suggest about the reasons that Lincoln embraced emancipation as a Union war aim?

From F. B. Carpenter, *Six Months in the White House with Abraham Lincoln* (New York: Hurd and Houghton, 1866), 75–77.

6.10 ABRAHAM LINCOLN TO CHARLES D. ROBINSON (AUGUST 17, 1864)

Charles D. Robinson was a Democratic newspaper editor from Green Bay, Wisconsin. Robinson supported the war effort, and (with misgivings) he had supported emancipation as a necessary war measure. Robinson grew concerned, however, by reports that Lincoln had made the abandonment of slavery a precondition for peace talks intended to bring a negotiated end to the rebellion. In August 1864, Robinson wrote Lincoln seeking clarification as to whether the abolition of slavery had become a Union war aim. Lincoln wrote a response to Robinson but appears to have not sent it.

GUIDING QUESTIONS:

1. Why does Lincoln tell Robinson he decided to issue the Emancipation Proclamation?
2. Why does Lincoln tell Robinson the Emancipation Proclamation cannot be rescinded?

LINCOLN TO CHARLES D. ROBINSON

HON. CHARLES D. ROBINSON EXECUTIVE MANSION,

WASHINGTON, AUGUST 17, 1864.

My dear Sir:

Your letter of the 7th. was placed in my hand yesterday by Gov. Randall.

To me it seems plain that saying re-union and abandonment of slavery would be considered, if offered, is not saying that nothing else or less would be considered, if offered. But I will not stand upon the mere construction of language. It is true, as you remind me, that in the Greeley letter of 1862, I said: "If I could save the Union without freeing any slaves I would do it; and if I could save it by freeing all the slaves I would do it; and if I could save it by freeing some, and leaving others alone I would also do that." I continued in the same letter as follows: "What I do about slavery and the colored race, I do because I believe it helps to save the Union; and what I forbear I forbear because I do not believe it would help to save the Union. I shall do less whenever I shall believe what I am doing hurts the cause; and I shall do more whenever I shall believe doing more will help the cause." All this I said in the utmost sincerety; and I am as true to the whole of it now, as when I first said it. When I afterwards proclaimed emancipation, and employed colored soldiers, I only followed the declaration just quoted from the Greeley letter that "I shall do more whenever I shall believe doing more will help the cause." The way these measures were to help the cause, was not to be by magic, or miracles, but by inducing the colored people to come bodily over from the rebel side to ours. On this point, nearly a year ago, in a letter to Mr. Conkling, made public at once, I wrote as follows: "But negroes, like other people, act upon motives. Why should they do anything for us if we will do nothing for them? If they stake their lives for us they must be prompted by the strongest motive—even the promise of freedom. And the promise, being made, must be kept." I am sure you will not, on due reflection, say that the promise being made, must be broken at the first opportunity. I am sure you would not desire me to say, or to leave an inference, that I am ready, whenever convenient, to join in re-enslaving those who shall have served us in consideration of our promise. As matter of morals,

From Roy P. Basler, ed., *The Collected Works of Abraham Lincoln*, vol. 7 (New Brunswick, NJ: Rutgers University Press, 1953), 499–501.

could such treachery by any possibility, escape the curses of Heaven, or of any good man? As matter of policy, to announce such a purpose, would ruin the Union cause itself. All recruiting of colored men would instantly cease, and all colored men now in our service, would instantly desert us. And rightfully too. Why should they give their lives for us, with full notice of our purpose to betray them? Drive back to the support of the rebellion the physical force which the colored people now give, and promise us, and neither the present, nor any coming administration, can save the Union. Take from us, and give to the enemy, the hundred and thirty, forty, or fifty thousand colored persons now serving us as soldiers, seamen, and laborers, and we can not longer maintain the contest. The party who could elect a President on a War & Slavery Restoration platform, would, of necessity, lose the colored force; and that force being lost, would be as powerless to save the Union as to do any other impossible thing. It is not a question of sentiment or taste, but one of physical force, which may be measured, and estimated as horsepower, and steam power, are measured and estimated. And by measurement, it is more than we can lose, and live. Nor can we, by discarding it, get a white force in place of it. There is a witness in every white mans bosom that he would rather go to the war having the negro to help him, than to help the enemy against him. It is not the giving of one class for another. It is simply giving a large force to the enemy, for nothing in return.

In addition to what I have said, allow me to remind you that no one, having control of the rebel armies, or, in fact, having any influence whatever in the rebellion, has offered, or intimated a willingness to, a restoration of the Union, in any event, or on any condition whatever. Let it be constantly borne in mind that no such offer has been made or intimated. Shall we be weak enough to allow the enemy to distract us with an abstract question which he himself refuses to present as a practical one? In the Conkling letter before mentioned, I said: "Whenever you shall have conquered all resistance to the Union, if I shall urge you to continue fighting, it will be an apt time then to declare that you will not fight to free negroes." I repeat this now. If Jefferson Davis wishes, for himself, or for the benefit of his friends at the North, to know what I would do if he were to offer peace and re-union, saying nothing about slavery, let him try me.

DRAWING CONCLUSIONS:

1. What does this letter suggest about the reasons that Lincoln embraced emancipation as a Union war aim?

AFRICAN AMERICAN SPIRITUALS

Among the most valuable sources for studying black perspectives on the war and emancipation can be found in African American spiritual songs. Spiritual songs focused on religious themes and were an important part of black culture under slavery. Such songs would be sung at prayer meetings, in the fields as people worked, and at other times. The songs and their lyrics would evolve as they were passed from person to person and from place to place. Themes of liberation were central to slave spirituals, and the figure of Moses (God's emissary who, in the story of the Exodus, freed the Israelite slaves from their bondage in ancient Egypt) loomed especially large. During the Civil War, a number of these spirituals evolved to focus more explicitly on slavery and emancipation, providing us with revealing perspectives on how slaves viewed the war and the prospect of their own liberation from bondage.

These African American spirituals are available to us through the efforts of individuals who heard these songs sung and wrote down the lyrics. (In some cases, these individuals also provided records of the melodies using musical notation.) Those who recorded these lyrics often used word spellings designed to reflect the dialects of the African American South.

7.1 "WE'LL SOON BE FREE"

The lyrics of this spiritual come to us from Thomas Wentworth Higginson, a white Massachusetts abolitionist who, in August 1862, was given command of a Union regiment operating on the South Carolina coast comprised of escaped slaves from the state. Higginson had a deep interest in the music of the black South, and he documented the lyrics of numerous spirituals. He also sought out information from his troops and from other people about the origins of these songs. Higginson was told that this song had been sung by a group of slaves in the town of Georgetown, South Carolina, just as the war was beginning (well before the Emancipation Proclamation was issued). Those singing it had been jailed on account of the song's subversive content.

GUIDING QUESTIONS:

1. What do the lyrics of this song suggest about the expectations for freedom of those who were singing it?

WE'LL SOON BE FREE

"We'll soon be free,
We'll soon be free,
We'll soon be free,
When de Lord will call us home.
My brudder, how long,
My brudder, how long,
My brudder, how long,
'Fore we done sufferin' here?
It won't be long (Thrice.)
'Fore de Lord will call us home.
We'll walk de miry road (Thrice.)
Where pleasure never dies.

We'll walk de golden street (Thrice.)
Where pleasure never dies.
My brudder, how long (Thrice.)
'Fore we done sufferin' here?
We'll soon be free (Thrice.)
When Jesus sets me free.
We'll fight for liberty (Thrice.)
When de Lord will call us home."

DRAWING CONCLUSIONS:

1. What does this song suggest about the impact that the outbreak of war had for those who were enslaved and their hopes for the future?

From Thomas Wentworth Higginson, *Army Life in a Black Regiment* (Boston: Fields, Osgood, and Company, 1870) 217–218.

7.2   "MANY THOUSAND GO"

This song was composed in South Carolina at some point during the war and was documented by Thomas Wentworth Higginson as well. This song was sung by black soldiers in Higginson's regiment. The terms "peck of corn" and "pint of salt" in the song refer to measurements of the two food items that slaves typically received as rations.

GUIDING QUESTIONS:

1. What do the lyrics of this song suggest about how the soldiers in Higginson's regiment viewed the issues at stake in the Civil War?

MANY THOUSAND GO

"No more peck o' corn for me,
No more, no more,—
No more peck o' corn for me,
Many tousand go.
"No more driver's lash for me, (Twice.)
No more, &c.
"No more pint o' salt for me, (Twice.)
No more, &c.
"No more hundred lash for me, (Twice.)
No more, &c.

"No more mistress' call for me,
No more, no more,—
No more mistress' call for me,
Many tousand go."

DRAWING CONCLUSIONS:

1. What can we learn from this song about liberated slaves' views of the war and of emancipation?

From Thomas Wentworth Higginson, *Army Life in a Black Regiment* (Boston: Fields, Osgood, and Company, 1870), 218.

7.3 "GO DOWN MOSES"/"FATHER ABRAHAM"

During the Civil War, the pre-war spiritual "Go Down, Moses" evolved to have a more explicitly political message. The key passage of the earlier version made reference to the biblical story of the Exodus. A Civil War-era version of this same spiritual recast Abraham Lincoln in role of Moses with Confederate President Jefferson Davis playing the role of Pharaoh.

GUIDING QUESTIONS:

1. In the Civil War version of this song, what meaning is conveyed by casting Lincoln in the role of Moses and Davis in the role of Pharaoh?
2. How is Abraham Lincoln portrayed in this song?

GO DOWN MOSES

(PRE-WAR VERSION)

"Oh! Go down, Moses
Go down into Egypt's land;
Tell King Pharaoh
To let my people go."

FATHER ABRAHAM

(CIVIL WAR VERSION)

Oh! Fader Abraham,
Go down into Dixie's land;
Tell Jeff. Davis

To let my people go.
Down in de house of bondage
Dey have watch and waited long,
De oppressor's heel is heavy,
De oppressor's arm is strong
Oh, Fader Abraham," etc.

DRAWING CONCLUSIONS:

1. What does this song suggest about the issues that African American people saw at stake in the Civil War?
2. What does this song suggest about African American views of Abraham Lincoln and his role in emancipation?

From David Macrae, *The Americans at Home: Pen-and-Ink Sketches of American Men, Manners, and Institutions* (Glasgow, Scotland: John S. Marr and Sons, 1875), 285–286.

ADDITIONAL RESOURCES

Bennett, Lerone Jr. *Forced into Glory: Abraham Lincoln's White Dream*. Chicago: Johnson Publishing Company, 2000.

Berlin, Ira et al., eds. *Slaves No More: Three Essay on Emancipation and the Civil War*. Cambridge: Cambridge University Press, 1992.

Brasher, Glenn David. *The Peninsula Campaign and the Necessity of Emancipation*. Chapel Hill: University of North Carolina Press, 2012.

Cox, Lawanda. *Lincoln and Black Freedom: A Study of Presidential Leadership*. Columbia: University of South Carolina Press, 1981.

Foner, Eric. *The Fiery Trial: Abraham Lincoln and American Slavery*. New York: W.W. Norton, 2010.

Gary W. Gallagher, *The Union War*. Cambridge, MA: Harvard University Press, 2011.

Chandra Manning, *What This Cruel War Was Over: Soldiers, Slavery, and the Civil War*. New York: Alfred A. Knopf, 2007.

Masur, Kate. *An Example for All the Land: Emancipation and the Struggle Over Equality in Washington, D.C.* Chapel Hill: University of North Carolina Press, 2010.

Masur, Louis P. *Lincoln's Hundred Days: The Emancipation Proclamation and the War for the Union*. Cambridge, MA: Harvard University Press, 2012.

McPherson, James M. "Who Freed the Slaves?" In *Drawn with the Sword: Reflections on the American Civil War* (New York: Oxford University Press, 1996).

Neely, Mark E. Jr. *The Last Best Hope on Earth: Abraham Lincoln and the Promise of America*. Cambridge, MA: Harvard University Press, 1995.

Oakes, James. *Freedom National: The Destruction of Slavery in the United States, 1861–1865*. New York: W.W. Norton, 2013.

Striner, Richard. *Father Abraham: Lincoln's Relentless Struggle to End Slavery*. New York: Oxford University Press, 2006.

Varon, Elizabeth R. *Armies of Deliverance: A New History of the Civil War*. (New York: Oxford University Press, 2019)

INDEX

Note: In this index, italic page numbers denote maps or art.